CIDER WIT

*A Walk Around the Borders of Somerset
with a Longdog*

Paul Hending

Cider with Roxie

ISBN 978-0-9568532-2-6

First Published August 2018

By Suffix

Forge House, Ansell Road,

Dorking, Surrey RH4 1UN

This book is dedicated to all those who collaborated in this hugely enjoyable exercise but, especially, to Geoff and to Roxie the Longdog

Contents

Prologue

(I've called this 'Prologue', rather than 'Introduction', not to be pretentious but because people often skip Introductions, and I really think you should read this if you're going to read the book at all.)

As the subtitle suggests, this book describes a series of walks which took me and Roxie the Longdog[1] all around the border of the county of Somerset. For no particular reason we chose the anti-clockwise direction and spread the walks over a period of about eighteen months, as and when time permitted. On all but a couple of them we were accompanied by various friends (see Cast List) whose contributions by way of good humour, navigational assistance and tolerance really can't be overstated. The two or three solo efforts, even with Roxie's company, were nothing like as much fun.

Starting from Brean Down in the autumn of 2013 we followed the coast to the Devon border at Glenthorne, then scaled the dizzy heights of Exmoor, Brendon and the Blackdowns before tracking the boundary line down to the rolling grasslands around Chard in Somerset's Deep South. From there we headed northwards via Yeovil and Wincanton in the Far East, then through the woods to Frome and Farleigh Hungerford in the north-east corner. Finally, we turned westward across glorious Mendip, returning to the mouth of the River Axe, near our starting point, in August 2015. These walks have served to confirm my belief that Somerset is the most beautiful and certainly the most varied county in England. And there's cider too.

The result is a collection of impressions of the borderlands of my home county. It is by no means a West Country attempt to emulate the worthy Wainwright's precision guides to the Lake District: if you should feel inclined to follow any of these walks you would be well advised to arm yourself with a map[2], compass, sat-nav device and, possibly, some prayers and good-luck charms, as my navigation has sometimes been less than precise.   Nor is it a lofty, scholarly travelogue laced with philosophical whimsy and impressive name-drops in the manner of a Chatwin, Deakin or Macfarlane.   It is, instead, a ground-level view of the outer edges of this beautiful county, not altogether ignoring a few less than beautiful bits, with a few stories and opinionated rants thrown in.

The course of the border has changed here and there over time, the most recent and the most drastic being on the 1st April 1974 when piratical bureaucrats decided it would be a good idea to purloin a chunk of north Somerset and stick it onto a similarly thieved bit of Gloucestershire to form the abomination they called 'Avon'. Even the pronunciation was a problem: Those who knew no better, including some of the bureaucrats, came out with 'Ave-on', as in the door-to-door cosmetics pedlars while, in fact, this cooked-up non-county was named after the river which formerly marked our northern boundary i.e. 'Ave-un', with the stress on the first syllable.

 We can only assume that someone, somewhere gained something from this outlandish pseudo-county. It has been suggested that it was a ruse to increase revenue to support the tax-guzzling metropolis of Bristol but, whatever the reason, the nonsensical fantasy which was 'Avon' bit the dust on 1st April in 1996. About time, you might say, but what happened next? Instead of returning the stolen bits to their respective counties, the powers-that-be cooked up four 'unitary authorities', the two which were formerly in Somerset being designated 'North Somerset' and 'Bath and North East Somerset' (BANES for short, appropriately enough).   Whilst these two anomalies are now within the 'ceremonial' county of Somerset, whatever that means, for practical purposes they are as far removed from us as was the nonsense-formerly-known-as Avon. For the purposes of this book I have, with regrets, confined myself to the current 'official' border, at least until such time as our northern-territories are liberated. (You see what I mean about "opinionated rants"?)

Another striking border change took place some-time just prior to 1787 when Somerset appears to have annexed from Devon a portion of Exmoor, resulting in the peculiar 'notch' in the north-west corner of our county. My explorations of the County Records Offices (both Somerset and Devon) and the National Archive have failed to explain how and why this bit of colonisation took place, so if there are any historians out there who can shed some light on this acquisition I should be delighted to hear from them. Similarly, the incorporation of the parish of Churchstanton on the Blackdowns into Somerset from Devon in 1896 remains unexplained, though doubtless welcomed by the inhabitants.   Several inexplicable 19th century losses to Dorset are further confirmation that messing about with county boundaries for no apparent reason is nothing new.

The total length of the county boundary has, therefore, changed a little from time to time, but is currently 286 miles (460km) according to BBC Radio Somerset, including about 40 miles (64 km) of coastline. I have no idea how far we actually walked in the course of this venture but, with back-tracks and deviations, it must have exceeded 300 miles by a fair step.   Along parts of its length the county boundary follows rivers or other geographical features, but in others its course seems pretty random.   Possibly these meanderings follow the boundaries of fiefdoms or manors of ancient times, when land holdings were established and maintained by the sword rather than by the bureaucrat's pen or the lawyer's will and testament. Following the borderline exactly has not always been possible, especially where it runs along busy roads or crosses 'private' land lacking Rights of Way, but we have mostly managed to stay within a mile or so, sometimes venturing across into the bordering counties of Devon, Dorset and Wiltshire.

Somerset as an entity was recognised by the Anglo-Saxons in the Chronicle of AD845, the name probably deriving from the

Sumorsaete, the tribe occupying the area after the native Britons had finally been driven out. It would be nice to think that these 'Summer People' were so called after their sunny dispositions, but the name probably refers to their habit of occupying the lowlands only in the summer and retreating to the hills in the wetter months. It seems likely that the county as a formal administrative area was established by the Normans, when William the Bastard was keen to divide England into neat parcels and hand them out to his cronies for safe keeping. It is surely quite remarkable that much of the land appropriated at that far-off time remains in the hands of the recipients' descendants to this day, including the Crown and the Church.

I make no apology for my antipathy towards these institutions, nor for the use of both Imperial and Metric units in the descriptions of our routes. As a rule, I have used miles and yards for horizontal distances and metres for the verticals, the former because I like them and the latter in keeping with current OS maps. This seemed to make sense, to me at least. So, with all that out of the way let's get on with the trip.

---

[1] The terminology regarding lurchers, sight-hounds etc. is, I think, pretty flexible except among freaky purists, but a Longdog, like Roxie, is generally taken to be a cross between two sight-hounds. eg. Greyhound x Deerhound, which is Roxie's supposed parentage. There is always the chance, though, that a bit of collie of one sort or another might have sneaked in there somewhere back along the line, in which case she would qualify as a lurcher. ie. Sight-hound with at least a dash of collie. Clear? (The idea of the collie x is to impart the 'brains' of the collie to the pace of the sight-hound. A vain hope in Roxie's case, alas.)

[2] OS maps 153, 140, OL9, 114,128, 115, 116, 129, 142, 141, more or less in that order, should cover it.

Cast: In Order of Appearance

Roxie (aka The Longdog): Beautiful deerhound/greyhound cross with, perhaps, a dash of collie. A dogged, if sometimes grumpy and sometimes lawless, companion from start to finish.

Chris: (sometimes with his belligerent whippet-lurcher Lottie, sadly no longer with us.) Ex-colleague and long-time friend. Keen naturalist and sometimes-whimsical observer of the world. Veteran of all but one of the coastal sections and the epic Brendons bash.

Miranda: Good friend, doctor and compassionate counsellor. (Thankfully, neither of these skills was called for on the treks.) Splashed through one of the coastal sections then came back for more in the Far East.

Geoff: Irishman, mathematician, author, addicted traveller and seafarer, and an old comrade from Zambia days. Stalwart of Exmoor, the Deep South, the Far East and middle Mendip sections as well as the Last Lap. (Sucker for punishment?)

Ginny: Geoff's wife. Unfortunately unable to join us on the earlier walks due to injury, but nobly chauffeured us to the farthest of the Far East and recovered in time for the Last lap.

Howard: Yorkshireman (no need to say more), accomplished lifter of dogs over gates and long-standing friend and colleague from Zambia days. Re-lived old times in the bush from Brendons to Blackdowns and middle Mendip sections.

Fraser: Self-deprecating musician, wit and genuine eccentric (though he would dispute the latter if not all three), and yet another old friend from long-ago Zambia days. Endured one of the longest treks, from Blackdowns to the Deep South, with characteristic good humour and unflagging interest.

Liisa: Fraser's Finnish wife. (Actually, his only wife.)   Kindly chauffeured us to the middle of nowhere.

Lorna: My ex-wife, and still the best of friends! Gallant companion on a couple of toughish North East sections, a bracken-bash over Mendip and the Last Lap, as well as a timely chauffeuse on more than one occasion.

The Twins: My confusingly-identical grandsons, Laurie and Joe, who romped across middle Mendip in grand style.

Lizzie: Nurse, actress, singer and more. My favourite ex-pupil and animal-rights activist. Accompanied me through the ascent and descent of west Mendip.

Pete: Recently-acquired naturalist/geographer, and the only native of Croydon in this celebrated company. Walked the first section of the R. Axe and reconnoitred the Last Lap, despite having 'dodgy knees' and little affinity with 'dawgs'.

Matti and Alexius: Dutch ex-Zambia friends who flew over from Kuala Lumpur via Holland to join us for the Last Lap, lending a splendidly international flavour to the finale.

My heart-felt thanks are due to all of them, for their companionship, good humour and forbearance.

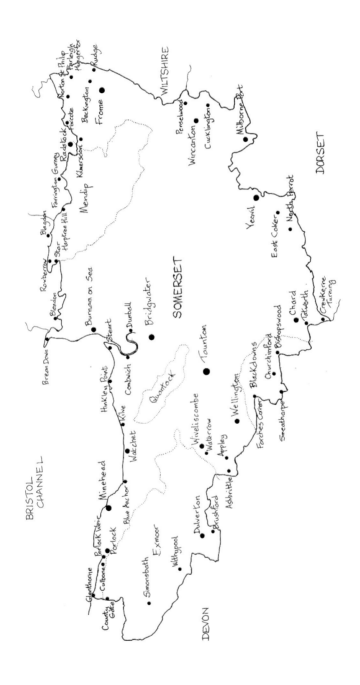

The Coast

Brean Down to Burnham

With Chris

If you will imagine for a minute the idea of a series of walks circumnavigating the border of the County, you will soon see that there is a potential problem in getting to and from the starting and finishing points of each section. You get to the starting point by some means or another, walk anything between ten and twenty miles in the day, and then what? As you'll see, we overcame these little difficulties in a number of ways with varying degrees of discomfort, but for the auspicious First in the series we thought we had it covered. This was the plan: we would drive to Burnham-on-Sea, catch a bus to Brean Down and, after circumnavigating the Down, walk back to Burham along the coast.

So it was that we found ourselves on a bright and beautiful autumn Sunday morning enjoying a coffee in a spacious, dog-friendly café on the promenade in pleasantly out-of-season Burnham. In contrast to the tourist-driven bustle of summer, the little town had the feel of an old cat stretching in the sun after a hard night and, as if to confirm the image, from the vantage point of the café we watched a not-so-young woman in a bathrobe emerge onto the balcony of a nearby apartment, stretch, and lean on the railing to gaze out across the shining estuarine mud.

Despite the pleasant view it was time to go. We sauntered across the road to the bus-stop and checked, again, the timetable which I'd painstakingly printed from the internet. Now, of all the infernal inventions that humankind has inflicted on the Earth, I rate the abominable internet as second only to the internal combustion engine in terms of damage done, and the forthcoming timetable experience did nothing to alter this view. According to my 'print out', Service No 112 would depart from Burnham at 10.11 and deposit us at Brean *village* some ten minutes later. This had been something of a disappointment in itself as it meant we would have to walk along the road from the village to the Down before starting on the proper border walk, but we could cope with that. (Why the 'off season' bus was unable to manage the final mile or so to the Down remains a mystery.) But the real disappointment was yet to come: the failure of Service 112 to appear at all. Some fifteen minutes or so after the appointed hour, as disquiet increased, a No 21 bound for Bridgwater appeared. The cheerful driver kindly considered my query and perused my proffered print-out with commendable professional interest. The indisputable fact that I had relied on an internet timetable seemed to induce a complex mixture of incredulity, merriment and pity as he explained the complete unreliability of these devices in general, and mine in particular. Despite the black and white evidence before us, he assured me that even if Service 112 had ever existed, a matter of some doubt, it would certainly not be running today. Grateful for his insight but more than a little disgruntled by his conclusion, we were obliged to abandon the bus idea, drive to the Down where the northern border meets the coast and take it from there. Roxie's first-ever bus ride would have to wait for another day.

Jutting out almost a mile westward into the Bristol Channel and 97m high at its peak, Brean Down is nothing less than awesome, in the original sense, the imposing cliffs of its southern flank towering over us as we approached from beach-level. We were faced with a choice of two routes for the ascent of the Down: the steep, unforgiving steps which climb straight up the side, or the rather more gentle, sloping path which angles up toward the east end. In deference to Roxie's dislike of steps, we chose the path up through the scrubby woodland which must provide a tangled haven for migrating birds in the spring. Stopping for a breather at a wooden platform about half-way up we looked out over glorious views to the south and west, taking in the Quantocks, Brent Knoll and even Glastonbury Tor in the distance, with the mysterious hazy flatlands in between.

At the top, only slightly out of breath, we crossed a close-cropped sward to reach the west-bound path on the northern side, where a long, gentle slope clad in bracken, brambles and wind-bent hawthorns runs down to the relatively low cliffs facing Weston Bay. The receding tide had revealed the course of the snaky R. Axe cutting its way across the mud and marking the border between us and notional 'North Somerset ', while the elegant Victorian frontage of Weston-super-Mare, elegant from this distance at least, sparkled on the other side of the Bay. As the cliffs are a long way off, Roxie was released from the lead and loped off ahead. We met surprisingly few walkers up here, but one friendly couple with a rather nervous whippety lurcher stopped for a chat, as hound people usually do. Having discussed the merits of sight-hounds in general and ours in particular we concluded, entirely without prejudice, that they are the finest of dogs, despite their occasional atrocities.   Roxie came cantering back to assess the fun potential but finding the little one reluctant to play she sloped off in disgust and continued her investigations of the undergrowth.

After another half-mile along the well-maintained gravel track we arrived at the fort at the western end of the Down. This ugly edifice, sometimes known as Palmerston's Folly after its original creator, was completed in 1877 at the behest of Queen Victoria herself, who was paranoid about the military intentions of the French with their recently acquired iron-clad warship. Seven huge guns were installed to discourage naval incursions up the Channel and, with typical

Victorian overkill, their enormous shells could penetrate 8-inch armour at a range of 1000 yards. Surely even French ships didn't carry that sort of protection? But those great guns never spoke in anger, as in 1900 one Gunner Haines discharged his rifle into the armoury in a fit of pique, detonating tons of gunpowder and blowing away half the fort as well as himself. Amazingly, no other lives were lost, but the fort was abandoned nevertheless. The fortification was rebuilt in WWII and, thankfully, never saw any action then either, but was used for trials of 'experimental' weapons. These included a 'bouncing' bomb which failed to bounce, and a catapult-launched missile which propelled itself ignominiously into the sea, catapult and all, at 200 mph before ending up in a nearby farmyard. Altogether, it has to be said that Brean Down Fort has a less than distinguished military record.

We turned our backs on the dismal concrete buildings and climbed the steep, grassy hill behind the Fort to the high-point of the Down. In the fierce breeze the 360° view was almost literally breathtaking, running from the Welsh coast through Steep Holm, Flat Holm, Weston, the Mendips, the Quantocks, Exmoor and back to the coast at Minehead, from what must be one of the finest vantage points in Somerset. In summer the close-cropped grassland on these southern slopes carries a whole range of specialised limestone plants including the rare White Rock-rose, Somerset Hair Grass and Wild Thyme, and we wondered, hopefully, if the latter might provide suitable habitat for the lovely Large Blue butterfly which has established itself in other parts of Mendip.

The south-side cliffs were far too close and high for canine comfort so Roxie was securely leashed as we strolled back along the spine of the Down over the sheep- and rabbit-nibbled grass. We stopped for lunch on the cliff-top at the eastern end and looked down on swarms of gulls and waders scattered over the shimmering mudflats bordering the Axe. Just below us on the face of the cliff we spotted a couple of shaggy, feral goats with huge horns taking their ease on patches of grass among the boulders, and Roxie, resigned to the confines of the leash, eyed them mournfully before flopping down beside me for her share of the sandwiches. Suitably restored, we left this idyllic picnic spot with more than a little reluctance and descended the path back to the car park which was by now almost full. Beautiful as it is, this must be a hellish place in summer, when cars and tourists will surely outnumber the gulls, waders and goats put together.

At this point we were faced with a small problem: our original intention, if you remember, was to bus it here from Burnham and walk back along the beach, but the mysterious absence of No. 112 compelled us to drive. Accepting that one mile of sandy beach is much the same as another, even if it is the border, we made the decision to compromise, and drove back to the small car-park at Berrow Dunes nature reserve. From there we aimed to walk along the coast to Burnham then return to the car by whatever means the map and our energy resources suggested. When I was a boy this windswept, marram-clad coastal flatland had its own bleak, spectral beauty, but more recent 'developments' have produced a neon-flashing, caravan-packed nightmare epitomised by the outlandish Congo Crazy Golf course with its monstrous plastic gorilla! Whilst I have a grudging understanding of the economic benefits of tourism, surely this atrocity is a primate too far.

From the car-park we took the sandy path running across the dunes between dense thickets of spiny Sea Buckthorn leading to the beach, 180° of gleaming sand and mud speckled with people and dogs. The forlorn wooden ribs of an ancient wreck protruding from the mud further down mark the spot where a Norwegian barque met her end in 1897, showing that even after a thousand years these Vikings never seem to learn. (cf. Combwich and Bleadon walks.) On the landward side, the face of the dunes, topped by marram grass and more buckthorn, had been hacked into sandy cliffs by recent storms and high tides, leaving a ragged stack of debris along the tide-line.

It is hard to reconcile this salty savagery with the gently sloping beach and the flat sea a mile away.

Another half an hour of uneventful beach trudging brought us back to the outskirts of Burnham-on-Sea, the town of three light-houses. The most apparent of these from the beach is the bold, red and white wooden structure, 11m high, standing on stilts in front of us on the sand. It was built in 1832, apparently as a supplement to the rather ineffectual 30m stone tower which stands about 100 yards inland. The latter was also built in the 1830's to replace the original Round Tower, which dates from the late 18th century and looks like a tiny castle. Both are now in residential rather than nautical use, leaving only the wooden oddity currently winking its eye at passing mariners. This proliferation of light-houses, none of them strikingly effective, somehow illustrates the half-assed workings of local authorities and 'authorities' in general through the ages, up to and including the present day.

With the coastal stretch completed we were faced with the necessity of getting back to the car at Berrow Dunes, preferably avoiding the defeatist option of simply retracing our steps. After cursing the bus companies and the internet once again we consulted the map and found a footpath running back along the top of the beach behind the dunes. This seemed like a good bet at the time, so we headed inland a little way and turned north at the southern end of Berrow golf course. At least this was conventional golf, with no reference to gorillas or other exotic animals. But in a small field next to the club-house we watched in awe as a lone man whacked golf balls, one after the other, into the distance, perhaps as some form of therapy? The area in front of him was heavily sprinkled with hundreds, maybe thousands, of balls, some close by and others far away, looking like a carpet of button mushrooms. Could this be another interpretation of Crazy Golf?

The sloshy footpath wound its way through a rank woodland strip between the golf course on the seaward side and the backsides of an endless row of suburban bungalows on the other. At one point the path became a lake hemmed in by savage brambles, so there was no choice but to take to the water. It is no great joy to endure water-filled boots, so it was with some relief that we scrambled onto the wooden causeway at the end of the pool where Roxie, wet to the elbows, shook herself vigorously and eyed me reproachfully. She seemed to be reflecting our own thoughts, saying, "Why wasn't that bloody causeway 20 yards longer?"

The swamp disgorged us onto the golf course where we were sternly warned of the dangers of flying balls by a troupe of humourless golfers, so we took cover, breaking through a barrier of dead Sea Buckthorn with some effort and minor blood-loss to regain the soggy bridleway leading to Berrow church. This typically squat, square-towered coastal place of worship was, apparently, first built in the 13th century, with the tower added some two hundred years later. Extensive restoration in the 19th century must have been done with more than usual Victorian sensitivity, as the place retains the look of considerable antiquity and quiet charm. Its most striking feature, for me at least, was the unusual extent of the well-filled graveyard, which appears to be well out of proportion to the compact church and the limited population hereabouts. There must have been a lot of death round here over the years. Another feature is the bold sign which reads "There Is No Lead On This Roof", and I am bound to wonder if churches are permitted to tell fibs.

The footpath/bridleway ends here, so we were forced to take to the road. Oh dear! Here we have strip 'development' at something approaching its worst, with a ribbon of ugly (if expensive) 1950's, 60's, 70's and probably more recent houses lining the road and obscuring completely the open flatlands beyond. The view of the sea is equally blocked by the high bank and the dunes on the other side of the road, so we endured the impression of being in a grim tunnel. Whilst it lacks the brash vulgarity of Brean's holidayland it was no less soulless, and utterly dismal in the fading light. About half way along the pavement disappeared so we engaged in the invigorating sport of car-dodging to relieve the tedium until, at last, and gratefully, we reached the safety of the Dunes car-park.

We reclaimed the car and drove back to our starting point at Burnham for a last off-the-lead run on the beach, where the metallic, late-afternoon light monochromed the endless, boundaryless sand, mud and water into a silvery daguerreotype. Chris and Roxie both managed to find a patch of Burnham's famous bottomless, squelchy mud, unmarked other than by their knee-deep footprints, and as we returned muddily to the car Chris remarked that "... this may well turn out to be the most beautiful and the most ugly of our walks, all in one." (I thought he might have been right at the time but, as it turns out, he wasn't.)

Burnham on Sea to Dunball Wharf along the River Parrett.

With Chris

This, the second coastal stage, begins at Burnham on Sea and follows the estuary of the River Parrett, so the plan this time was to leave the car at Dunball on the river, bus it to Burnham and walk back to Dunball. We could only hope that this bus service is more accommodating than the last one. I think the actual border is somewhere out in the Bristol Channel, so the nearest we can get, without resorting to a boat, is to follow the coastline. (I'm not sure of the extent of our Territorial Waters out there, but I hope they are rigorously enforced.)

The roadside at Dunball Wharf is hardly the loveliest spot in Somerset, hemmed in by a roaring dual carriageway and backed by looming factory units, but the short wait for the bus was relieved by a brace of elderly Eastern European gentlemen also waiting at the bus stop. The English-speaking member of this unlikely pair expressed great admiration for Roxie then regaled us with tales of his own far-away hounds. I was particularly impressed by the story of his Doberman, a dog of such sweet temper that with uncomplaining stoicism it tolerated the old gentleman's little grandson applying a pair of pliers to its tail. Some interesting and unlikely tales are to be encountered at bus stops.

To our delight if not surprise the bus arrived as predicted, and Roxie glided on board for her first-ever bus journey as if to the manner born. Longdogs may, just occasionally, have their drawbacks but, when it comes to aplomb, they are in a class of their own. The driver was not a communicative man but got us safely to Apex Leisure Park, where we were delighted to find Lizzie's Kitchen, a striking mobile catering unit in the form of a heavily-riveted, stainless-steel-clad caravan reminiscent of 1950's American automobiles. Their hot chocolate and dangerously-sweetened chocolate shortbread were not to be resisted so, suitably fortified, we stepped out on the second stage of our amble around Somerset.

The Apex lakes were alive with bread-fed ducks, swans, assorted geese and patrolling gulls as we followed the gravelled paths across the park and climbed a grassy bank onto the footpath heading inland along the north side of the River Brue. As the tide was still low, the great slabs of sloping grey/brown mud banks looked like wet elephant hide flanking the identically-coloured water. It is characteristic of these estuaries, the Brue, Parrett and Severn, that the water matches the mud banks exactly, the boundaries indistinguishable in the hard, bright sunlight. With the sewage works to the left and the outskirts of Highbridge up ahead, this is not, in itself, a pretty place, but the harsh light reflecting off the mud and the unbroken flat landscape gave an odd sensation of liberation and space. The breeze, brushing around a decaying fishing boat drawn well up above the tide mark, seemed to be whispering something about better times hereabouts, and bore out the general air of comfortably resigned dilapidation.

Having reached Highbridge (less said the better) we crossed the Brue over the road bridge and headed back west along its southern bank. As we approached its confluence with the Parrett we cut across the neck of an almost circular meander (soon to be an ox-bow straight out of a geography text book?) and joined the path running south down the eastern bank of the Parrett. Even with the tide rising fast the interminable glistening mud banks blurred the boundaries between the river, Steart Island to the north and Steart (or Stert) Point just across the water to the west, all in a shimmering haze. In response to the rising tide, clouds of displaced gulls, waders and ducks wheeled around like distant snowstorms as their low-water feeding grounds were gradually covered.

We reached the Huntspill river, which we crossed by way of the stark steel and concrete sluice which controls the water as it meets the Parrett. The Huntspill is, in fact, man-made, as is testified by its dead straight course. It was begun in 1940, primarily to supply the 4.5 million gallons of water needed daily by the Royal Ordnance Factory to manufacture munitions in WWII. Its ancillary function, to control flooding and maintain drainage on the Levels, continues to this day, though the ROF establishment, a few miles upstream, ceased production in 2008 after a series of dubious privatisations. Its new proposed role as a 'renewable energy park' is generally welcomed by the locals, whose washing on the line was frequently ravaged by chemical fall-out from the 'bomb factory', but dark rumours of storage facilities for the forthcoming nuclear power station extension at Hinkley Point are viewed with rather less enthusiasm. As we continued south on the footpath, very close to the Parrett's east bank, the dreaming spires or, rather, towers of the existing Hinkley installations became clearly visible some four or five miles to the west. At this distance their presence is hardly threatening, if decidedly ugly, but it is still hard to ignore the potential dangers lurking in their mysterious interiors.

Up ahead we made out a small van parked on the track, and a lone figure pottering about near the water's edge. As we approached he returned to the van and leant on the door waiting for us to arrive, perhaps curious, and certainly willing to engage in conversation.

This large, grizzled man, it turned out, is one of the last of the Parrett net-fishermen whose carefully-chosen pitch is one of the few places where the water can be approached safely, with rock underfoot instead of the bottomless mud. At this time of year, he told us, the catch is likely to be dabs (small flatfish) and, maybe, a few codling, but in the past the highlight of the season was the annual salmon run. In those days, at least a dozen local families supplemented their income with salmon fishing, but now the fish have all but gone. It seems incredible that the noble fish we associate with rushing clear water should fight its way through the cocoa-thick murk of the Parrett but, even this year we are told, about a dozen were reported upstream in the River Tone, one even reaching a tributary in Bishops Lydeard. I hear that salmon have returned even to the once-filthy Thames, so perhaps there's hope.

We bade our friendly fisherman good day and pressed on. Such are the meanderings of the Parrett that in the last few miles we have walked south, west and now due north following the bank of the river, which is all very disorientating as Hinkley Point, the pretty village of Combwich across the river, and the Quantock Hills in the distance all appeared to have moved round the points of the compass as we walked. As we followed the path around the flat, rhyne-locked fields of Pawlett Hams and stopped for a lunch break, the tide reached its peak and the mud had all but disappeared, with curlews, in ones and twos, beating downstream against the wind and fluting their mournful, defiant calls. Suddenly a blade-winged merlin, one of the delights of the day, flashed low across the fields over the heads of the grumpy-looking cattle. Through the winter this fierce little falcon, barely bigger than a thrush, plies its predatory trade with breath-taking panache over these coastal flatlands.

With a rather cursory lunch break over, a quick map check revealed that we were approaching Gaunt's Clyce. A 'clyce', and there are many of them along the tidal reaches of the Parrett, is a small man-made tributary which is gated or 'sluiced' to allow water to drain into the main river but which can be closed to prevent brackish incursions. The first of these was constructed early in the 13th century with numerous additions through to the 16th century, the effect being to convert the salt marshes into fresh-water bogs which could be used for summer grazing, as they are to this day.

Rounding the last major bend along the Parrett's tortuous course we could hear the first sounds of what some might call 'civilisation': the rumble of traffic on the A38 and M5 over to the east. We passed the old brickyard and its accompanying cottages, noticing that the cottages appear to stand well below the high-water mark behind their protecting wall which served as a dock for the boats which transported the bricks when the industry was thriving in the 19th and early 20th centuries.

 Making the final 90° turn to the east we could see Dunball Wharf half a mile or so up ahead. The wharf, which testifies to the navigability of the river up to this point, was built in 1844 by Bridgwater coal merchants, and certainly earned its keep in WWII when it received Welsh coal to supply the munitions factory. Now it is reduced to handling sand and gravel dredged out of the Bristol Channel but still, the huge dredgers off-loading at high tides make an impressive sight. The rest of the wharf has now been taken over by a range of unlovely factory units, dominated by a major recycling facility through which the footpath winds on its way back to our starting point.   Huge tangles of multi-coloured plastics and mountains of sand piled around the sharp-angled warehouses make the word 'incongruous' seem entirely inadequate to describe this surreal bit of estuarine landscape.

After a day of stiff southerly winds and brittle autumn sunshine the sky was clouding up menacingly over the stark industrial buildings. Against the bruised clouds an almost synthetically bright rainbow appeared suddenly and, if that wasn't a sufficiently spectacular end to the day, a lone peregrine falcon swung into view over the factory roofs, circling again and again through the rainbow.

So, this second stage of our Somerset border safari finished with a towering peregrine and a blazing rainbow across a leaden sky over a mud-thick high tide lapping against Dunball Wharf. Roxie had loped along happily all day exploring these unfamiliar, other-worldly flatlands, but now she was ready for a drink, and so was I.

Combwich to Hinkley Point, and back via Stockland Bristol and Otterhampton.

With Chris & Lottie

As we had walked the length of the Parrett estuary last time out we decided to skip the Bridgwater end and start the next leg downstream at Combwich on the way back to the Bristol Channel coast and the border. I should admit to feeling a certain guilt about 'skipping' Bridgwater, a much-maligned and derided little town of great and distinctive character but, as it is not really a border town, I felt justified in pressing on without it. (In the cause of fairness, Geoff and I strolled the towpath from the centre of Bridgwater to Combwich a few months later. Nothing to report, except perhaps the splendid stone-built bus-shelter at Combwich from which we successfully bussed it back to Bridgwater.)

The picturesque village of Combwich sits snugly on the west bank of the River Parrett some four miles from the river mouth as the curlew flies. (Nearer six as the river meanders.) It is an ancient settlement, its name, pronounced 'Cummitch', deriving from the Old English *cumb wic*, meaning 'settlement by the water', appropriately enough. Its best claim to historical fame is, perhaps, that the Viking raider Hubba and his crew were killed there in 878AD, demonstrating that Somersetians have never welcomed invaders, and helping to explain why the Danes failed to establish a lasting foothold on our south-western shores. From the 15th century Combwich became a thriving port, mostly for coal and the products of the local brick and tile industries, but the trade declined, the creek silted up in the 1930's and that was the end of that. Today the little harbour provides a home for only a few leisure craft, but the threat/promise of traffic concerned with the latest Hinkley Point 'developments' may see a renewal in its commercial fortunes, for good or ill depending on your point of view.

We arrived on a pale grey, misty morning at low tide, with the spectacular mud-scapes of the Parrett estuary stretching away to the north. As we set out to walk downstream along the broad, gravelled track beside the river, flocks of Wigeon rose up from the far bank, the shepherds' whistles of the drakes underscored by the purring growl of the ducks. To the west the flat fields, cut through with rhynes, stretched away to the coast and, in the distance, the pale grey lump of the nearest Hinkley Point tower loomed out of the mist, sending a chain of huge pylons striding across the river just ahead of us. The mudbanks here are slashed with deep channels running down to the rippling, shifting water below, looking like elephant-grey versions of the erosion gullies on Ethiopian mountains. As there were no obvious dog hazards to be seen I unleashed an impatient Roxie, allowing her to lope ahead into the mist looking for trouble. We were graced with Chris's dog, Lottie, for this one but, mindful of past misdemeanours, Chris wisely kept her secured.

As we reached the pylons we recalled walking here last year when a single Crane flew low overhead at sunset; so low that we could clearly see its un-ringed legs, showing it to be a truly wild bird and not one of the Slimbridge-bred flock now in residence on the Levels. It is difficult to explain why the provenance of this fabulous 'wild' creature is significant, but there is no denying my added delight at noting its freedom from any association with Man.

Passing under the pylon line and crossing the North Clyce we could see the obvious signs of ongoing activity which will lead to the creation of new salt-marshes between the river and the coast towards Steart. Evidence of the extensive earthworks was everywhere: huge piles of spoil, ramps for the heavy machinery, new shallow lagoons bustling with wildfowl, and large 'Beware Pedestrians' signs. (We assumed these are to alert the digger drivers, but who knows, they may be a warning. This is Somerset after all, and we know what happened to Hubba.) This enormous saltmarsh nature reserve may become yet another jewel in Somerset's wildlife crown but, pondering the effects of these developments, we were bound to wonder how this long-standing wildlife haven will change when eventually completed. Will it become another bird-watchers' Piccadilly Circus like Ham Wall on the Levels where, it seems to me, you often see almost as many bird-watchers as birds, especially in the winter starling-roost season or when some hapless rarity turns up. If you enjoy shoulder-to-shoulder bird-watching, complete with tripods and bazooka 'scopes, then it's fine, but it's not for me. We fervently hope that this area never loses its wild, almost desolate beauty, and that the coach parties stay at Ham Wall.[1]

Chris, my stalwart companion again, was just ahead. "Deer", he hissed, and pointed to the left. Just in time I grabbed Roxie's collar and clipped on the leash. She spotted the retreating deer, a trio of elegant little Roe, and went completely wild, leaping in the air and twisting and turning to escape the martingaled (anti-choke) collar. Holding on to 32kg of hunt-crazed lurcher is, I imagine, rather like

---

[1] At the time of final writing the Steart Marshes Nature Reserve is more or less completed, with capacious hides, numerous signposts and miles of gravelled cycle tracks. It is as I feared but, whether I like it or not, the creation of a huge, new salt-marsh habitat is not to be denied.

trying to land a marlin or an outraged shark.   As the deer disappeared into the distance, bounding effortlessly over the rhynes as they went, the frantic Roxie gradually calmed down, but I thought it best to keep her on the leash for a bit, just in case, as a 4ft stock-fence topped with barbed wire is no obstacle for a Longdog on a mission. Chris's small, sleek lurcher simply barked once or twice out of solidarity but was otherwise unmoved by the deer or Roxie's display of savagery.

At this point we found the track along the top of the embankment to be closed off with a barrier bearing another Beware Pedestrians sign, so we took a last look at the vast, awe-inspiring expanses of low-tide estuarine mud before turning away from the river along a narrow, reed-lined path. After skirting a couple of damp, grassy fields we emerged onto the road which leads out to Steart (or Stert) Point. The hamlet of Steart is, I'm afraid, a dismal place. Over the decades I've been coming here I've seen it in sunshine, rain and snow, but even in this softening autumn light it is still a dismal place, the ranks of wooden battery houses adding their grim presence to its lack of charm. Ah well. Not everywhere in Somerset can be beautiful.

Turning north-east we approached Steart Point, a long-established nature reserve with artificial scrapes, reedbeds and pools to attract the birds, and an assortment of hides dotted about, including a monumental wooden tower. I can remember when the whole area was flat, unfenced and open, and dotted only with the remains of WWII defences in the form of glider traps: sturdy poles with cables strung between them. The War Ministry, as it was then, was convinced that Adolf's lot were going to invade via the West Country, which explains the glider-catchers, and the pill boxes you find everywhere from Bossington to the Taunton-Bridgwater canal and beyond. Perhaps the Enemy knew what happened to Hubba and his ill-fated crew, as the invasion never materialised.

We took an early lunch-break in one of the hides looking north toward Steart Island. The great hump of Steepholm rears out of the distant water to the west, and the monochrome panorama sweeps around, passing the Victorian splendour of Burnham sea-front, past Crook Peak and Brent Knoll and follows the far-off Mendips as they disappear into the mist to the south-east. If you are not moved by this mighty sweep of water, mudflats, islands and hills you are surely not a Somersetian, not even an honorary one.

Leaving the hide we started out on the second phase of our walk, heading west along the Bristol Channel coast towards Hinkley Point. The path follows a low pebble ridge with extensive reedbeds on the seaward side and small, sad-looking fields on the landward. When I was a boy the reedbeds were just a narrow fringe, the upper shore being covered with beds of Spartina grass, but over the years these have collected silt such as to raise the level enough for the reeds to colonise: a nice example of ecological succession in action.

The dubious path soon petered out, so we turned inland a short distance to a small car park. Here we found an odd sort of monument thing, perhaps someone's idea of a sculpture, made of slabs of blue lias with an incongruous pure white cast of a large ammonite stuck in the middle. I can't say it struck me as being in any way attractive or appropriate, but it bade us 'Welcome to Bridgwater Bay' and, apparently, marks the beginning (end?) of the West Somerset Coast Path. We left the car park and headed west along the road, passing the forlorn chicken sheds and one eye-sore of a modern house from which emerged, at speed, a villainous-looking collie. It hit the road and headed towards us with obvious ill-intent, but Roxie, fortunately on the lead, spun round and faced it with a superior sneer, and the collie wisely skidded to a halt and retreated. Two magpies flew across our path. "One for sorrow, two for joy," my old granny used to say. The day was blessed.

We left the road where it turns inland at Wall Common and took to the track. The saltmarsh between us and the coastal embankment bears a range of characteristic plants like Sea Lavender and Yellow-horned Poppy which were in flower when we were here a few months ago. The low-lying fields to our left are bordered by a long stone wall (hence Wall Common?) and we debated the purpose of this substantial boundary, unusual out here where the fields are bordered by rhynes and scraggy hedges. Our best theory, sea defence, is somewhat punctured by the presence of gates at regular intervals which, we concede, are rather less than waterproof. Another mystery unsolved. The path angles across the common, and we rejoined the embankment above the high-tide mark. The water was still miles away and, on the upper shore, clumps of Spartina valiantly continued their land reclamation programme, so perhaps this too will be reedbeds one day. Way out on the mudflats we could see rows of irregular poles set in lines, probably the signs of the last of the famous Bridgwater Bay mud-fishermen and their unique sledges. There was no sign of life out there, but we made a note to pursue the phenomenon of the mud-men later.

As we approached Stolford we noticed on the landward side of the bank a small wooden cross set with a brass plaque simply stating: "In Remembrance of 5 Polish Students. 15th July 1994", followed by a few words in Polish. What tragedy happened here almost twenty years ago? (Enquiries later revealed that five young Poles, students at the local agricultural college, were driving along this track on the fateful night. Their car came off the embankment and plunged into the adjacent rhyne, where they remained undiscovered until the following day. A tragedy indeed.)

The sea wall from here on is reinforced with huge rocks brought in from who-knows where to protect the low-lying fields behind and a scattering of at least six named farm houses within three or four square kilometres, according to the map. It's hard to imagine that many (or any) of these can make a living on such small acreages of pretty hostile land, so perhaps they are all 'second homes' or retirement refuges like so many Somerset properties these days. I could feel a rant coming on, so we moved on.

Hinkley Point B was looming directly ahead, humming menacingly. This is probably the least lovely aspect of a pretty unlovely edifice: a monstrous grey block towering over us. Perversely, we decided to stop for our second lunch on the rocks which are literally in the shadow of the monster where, years ago, someone optimistically planted countless trees inside the security fence, presumably as an attempt at a screen. Alas, even if they were giant redwoods, which they are not, they would have little hope of ever screening the massive lump of concrete overshadowing them.

Better to look seaward. This is the first point on our westward path where the Triassic/Jurassic blue lias strata are visible, the sloping pavements, clad with seaweed, stretching out in sweeping, concentric curves towards the incoming tide. About 100 yards to our left, between the exposed rocks, a spout of water suddenly appeared, and was repeated every minute or so. This looked rather like the natural 'blow holes' to be found in places on the Dorset and south Cornwall coast, but here the sea is still a long way out so we concluded that this one might have something to do with the power station outlets. A couple of hundred yards further out the water intake, or caisson, squats on the water's edge like a sinister miniature fortress, adding to the general air of menace. Before we lapsed into terminal melancholy our attention was thankfully distracted by the angry cries of a majestic peregrine falcon driving a hapless buzzard away. To the falcon's eye, I suppose, the towering concrete slab is just another convenient vantage point; another cliff, the incongruous ugliness of the edifice being irrelevant to the sky-searing bird.

Abandoning the border for the day, we turned our backs on the 'steaming spires' of Hinkley Point and headed off inland, glad to leave the hum behind. Our intention was to return to Combwich 'cross country' and, with hitherto unknown footpaths and fast-fading light, this had the makings of an interesting exercise. We began heading south on an easy path to the hamlet of Wick, a cluster of a few very pretty, heavily tarted houses around a picturesque brook and stone bridge. The path now appeared to follow the stream for a short distance before climbing up on the other side, allowing Roxie to skip daintily along the slippery bank while we floundered about in the mud.

And at this point the trouble started. The light was almost gone, the footpaths were indistinct and poorly marked and, approaching Stockland Bristol over flat, rhyne-divided fields, only a spot of good luck found us a sleeper bridge across the first significant channel. The next bridge was guarded by a makeshift stile topped with a couple of strands of baler twine, and in the semi-darkness Chris caught his foot and descended in less than elegant fashion. Although forewarned, I managed to follow suit and found myself hanging upside down with one foot well entangled. Chris kindly composed himself enough to extract the foot, and we hobbled up a long slope, the first sign of elevation for many a mile, towards the lights of the village. We scrambled through a hedge onto the road, found what we thought might be the appropriate footpath sign and set off across what appeared to be someone's garden. Thankfully undetected, we crossed a couple of fields and found ourselves overlooking a huge barn, ablaze with light. As we sneaked through the farmyard we passed close to the barn, which was stuffed full of dairy cattle packed like sardines. The ceaseless hum of automatic milking machines added to the horror of this awful place as we made our escape, wishing that these unfortunate beasts could do likewise.

On the Otterhampton road, in total darkness, we tried in vain to find a functional footpath, and I still wonder to myself why I failed to bring a torch. After wandering about in a nettle-filled field we resorted to Chris's electronic map thing to get us back to the Cannington-Hinkley road where the intermittent traffic with blinding headlights seemed almost certain to kill us all.   In desperation we resorted to the satnav thing again and, with Chris following the blue dot, we took to the fields. What Roxie made of all this I've no idea, but she loped along stoically, leaping whatever obstacles we encountered without complaint with Lottie plodding along in her wake.

By a combination of electronics and miracles we managed to hit a footpath and there, below, were the lights of Combwich. Triumphant, we strolled nonchalantly down the final field and emerged onto the Parrett Trail only a few yards from where we had started in the morning. The lights along the Channel, reflected in the now risen water, made a sensational display, sweeping along the Welsh coast, through Burnham like a rippling comet and ending with the piercing green markers on the Combwich quay. This was a truly memorable sight, and well worth the minor traumas which preceded it.

The Anchor Inn beckoned, and we (the dogs at least) received the deserved heroes' welcome. Rarely have ham and eggs and a pint tasted so good; a fitting end to a day of contrasts. We had seen the eternal beauty of the river and the coast, and the grim realities of Hinkley Point and a factory farm, all of which we must accept as part of the famous diversity of Somerset.

Interlude 1

Fishing, Somerset Style

The coast of Somerset is, for the most part, rocky and muddy, with a very shallow slope out into the Bristol Channel and the second highest tide range in the world. This unique combination of features means that the sea is barely visible at low tides, sliding away several kilometres into the distance towards Wales. In Bridgwater Bay this presents the opportunity for a couple of methods of fishing which are/were unique to Somerset, as far as I know.

The first, now no longer practised, is the ancient sport of glatting, an unusual method of hunting conger eels. The name comes from the German word 'glatt', meaning 'smooth and slippery', which became the local term for the conger eel, perhaps bearing witness to our Saxon ancestry.

At low spring tides, perversely mostly in autumn, the hunters and their glatting dogs would gather as far out as they dared go among the exposed rocks. Prints from the 19th century suggest that the dogs were originally Jack Russells or fox terriers, but 20th century photographs show spaniels and various retriever types. Whatever the breed, the dogs would seek out the eels hiding among the rocks, and the hunters would move in with long, ash poles to dislodge the boulders and reveal the fish. Once exposed, the congers would head for the sea at speed while the assembled company attempted to catch them with gaffs on the ends of the glatting poles. Big, slippery eels with an inclination to bite, equally slippery rocks and glutinous mud seem like a recipe for mayhem but that, I suppose, is sport of a kind. Old accounts describe the eels being shepherded into sacks, but a big conger is a fearsome beast capable of inflicting serious injury, so I suspect they were more usually killed on the spot.

Glatting was popular between the Wars when food was scarce, but the last recorded expedition was in 1955. Conger flesh is not highly esteemed among fishermen, so it is no surprise that this dangerous and not hugely productive sport died out when alternative sources of protein became more readily available.

Somerset's other unorthodox fishing technique is still operated from Stolford, where one family of mud-horse fishermen practise the arcane art which has passed down at least five generations. At one time in recent years about a dozen families supplemented their livings in this way, but now only the stalwart Sellicks remain custodians of the mud-horse tradition.

If you look out from the foreshore along this stretch of coast you will see rows of rough posts standing in lines way out on the mud. You may be able to make out the nets, which are strung between the posts at low water to await the incoming tide. At the next low tide the mud-horse fisherman treks out across the treacherous, boot-sucking mire pushing his trusty steed: The mud-horse is a large, wooden sledge with wide, flat runners and a superstructure designed to carry the buckets, sieves and nets which make up the fisherman's paraphernalia. Note that the sledge is pushed, not pulled, by the brawny fisherman leaning on the wheelbarrow-style handles at the back, thus supporting himself as well as propelling the beast forward. This is no game for the feeble or faint-hearted.

Adrian Sellick, the current exponent, knows the mud flats like the back of his hand, and traverses the mile or more to the nets in relative safety with the help of the gliding 'horse'. Once there, he empties the nets into a sieve and decants his catch into buckets and baskets. The fish species vary with the season, mainly whiting, cod and sprats in the winter replaced by sea bass, skate and ling in the summer. Brown shrimps, mostly taken in the autumn, are the most valuable catch, but their numbers have declined in recent years, perhaps due to the incessant depredations of the Hinkley Point water intake.

With the harvest safely on board, Mr Sellick propels the loaded mud-horse back up the gently sloping shore ahead of the incoming tide. The catch is processed with the help of his father, Brendan, the previous mud-horse fisherman, then mostly sold from their cottage at Stolford.

Adrian is in his fifties now, and his four children are all pursuing their own careers with no inclination to follow the tough calling of their forebears. But they have children of their own, and perhaps we might hope that one of these, one day, may take up the ancient mantle of the mud-horse fisherman.

Hinkley Point to Kilve and back

With Chris

Returning to Hinkley Point we parked the car in an informal lay-by a short distance from the main entrance to the nuclear power station, and as it must be well within range of their impressive security cameras we reckoned it should be pretty safe parking. Assembling dog and day-sacks we set off up the road to find the recently-diverted footpath, only to be confronted by a three-metre-high, barbed-wire-topped security fence stretching off into the distance. As we faced this daunting barrier a pick-up appeared on the inside and a cheerful, oriental security guard climbed out and came over to where I was holding on to the wire like a hapless POW. In response to our queries he patiently explained that to reach the coast we should follow the fence "a long way". Fair enough, so we set off along the fence, recently erected to protect the site of the proposed third reactor, the infamous Hinkley C.

The diverted footpath takes an oddly dog-legged course heading roughly west, and the man wasn't joking: it surely is 'a long way'. The fence encloses an enormous area to the west of the existing power stations, reputedly bought from the lucky landowner for £80 million, and we can only ponder how many new reactors 'they' intend to construct here. It looks as if there's room for half a dozen at least. Eventually the fence/path turns north towards the coast, and we descended into a steep-sided valley before climbing to a ridge overlooking the high tide, with the Welsh coast bright and clear across the water. The Somerset coast snakes away to the west, the solid lump of North Hill providing a scenic backdrop for the awful, incongruous white domes of what we used to call Butlin's holiday camp in the distance.

From our vantage point on the ridge we were treated to this glorious panorama which was only slightly marred by a couple of odd 'lampshades' hanging on a gibbet next to the path. These, Chris tells me, are dust-catchers which allow the denizens of the power station to monitor radiation levels. We tried to ignore their sinister implications as we marched off the ridge to the top of the first real cliffs we've yet encountered on this stretch of coast, where large, stern notices warn of Unstable Cliffs, and they mean it: The crumbling rubble of the Upper Jurassic forms wicked overhangs with plenty of evidence of recent collapses. (Roxie was securely on the leash at this point. One random rabbit is quite enough to suspend her already dubious sense of self-preservation, so we take no chances.) Looking back inland we could see the odd, spiky spire of Stogursey church stuck incongruously on top of its white-painted tower. The church dates from the 12th century but has been renovated and generally messed about many times since by local worthies trying to secure their places in heaven. On the rising field to our left a couple of roe deer stood stock still in silhouette against the pale sky, but Roxie failed to see them so they remained blissfully undisturbed.

The cliff top begins to slope down from here, so we ambled down to the pebble beach at Lilstock Outfall. We took a coffee break on the pebbles and watched a lone rod-fisherman engrossed in solitary vigil, his brace of rods pointing to the sky like aerials. I have watched many of these stalwarts along this whole stretch of coast over the years, yet I've never seen a single catch, and it would be interesting to know the average number of hours per fish, or some similar measure of their success. Perhaps I'm missing the point.

We were now somewhere near the middle of the great sweep of Bridgwater Bay, with cliffs rising to both east and west. The panorama is nothing short of breath-taking, from the big cliffs backing Minehead around to Flat Holm, Steep Holm and Brean Down sitting on the silky sea. Leaving Lilstock we tramped up the close-cropped grassy slope to regain the cliff top. Ahead is the prominent Range Quadrant Hut, so it says on the map, used by the RAF and/or the Fleet Air Arm to monitor their target practice in the Bristol Channel. The incongruous little white tower, some six or seven metres high, is protected by a serious security fence and looked to be well maintained, so we assume it to be still operational. I'm sure I've never seen its aerial accomplices in action, but it would certainly make a stirring sight.

We proceeded along The Gallop, formerly used to exercise race-horses, and looked down to the famous fossiliferous Kilve beach. The magnificent blue lias pavements were just being revealed by the retreating tide, but we resisted the temptation to hunt for ammonites as we will visit this beach again on the next leg of our coastal jaunt. Instead we turned inland past the car park where, on the left, a small, cylindrical brick building with some chimney-like metal-work stuck on the top caught the eye. This is the remains of one of several retorts built at the beginning of the 20th century in an attempt to extract oil from the bituminous shales found hereabouts. Although this stuff supposedly yielded up to 40 gallons of oil per cubic metre, the company was unable to raise sufficient finance, and the whole ghastly project was abandoned. If I were of a religious disposition I should shout "Thank God" at the top of my voice. The imagination shrivels at the thought of a foulsome oil refinery in this beautiful place, still relatively unspoilt despite the public toilets and parking meter.

We headed up the narrow road to Kilve village, passing the ruins of the 12th century chantry on the right. These mark the remains of a small monastery which was dissolved in the 14th century, around the time that a similar institution at Stogursey bit the ecclesiastical dust. These monastic foundations were often set up by the in-coming Norman barons (one de Furneaux in the case of Kilve) specifically to pray for the well-being of their benefactors. Presumably, by the 14th century the sponsors were running short of cash or, perhaps, no longer felt the need for supplication. After its religious demise the chantry was adopted by the locals and put to a more practical, secular purpose: as a 'warehouse' for the storage of contraband, for which this stretch of coast was rightly famous.

Next on the right is the church of St Mary the Virgin, rebuilt in the 14th century on the site of the Saxon original. Set in a lush, green churchyard this squat, white-painted place of worship has a pleasant, homely feel, as churches go.

The lane winds between an assortment of prettied-up cottages, dull bungalows and the occasional conversion/renovation atrocity. (The mysteries of planning permission in West Somerset are deep, indeed.) Just ahead is the main Bridgwater – Williton road and The Hood Arms, Roxie's former home, which we were, of course, duty bound to visit. As always, she greeted her erstwhile mentor with affection but, I'm pleased to note, she is up and ready to go as soon as we finished our pints and braced ourselves for the return trip.

We emerged into bright sunshine and began our return journey cross-country up a fiercely steep footpath set in a narrow gulley. We ascended about 50 metres vertically, according to the map, then stepped out onto the aptly-named Hilltop Lane, where the view in all directions is nothing short of stunning. With the splendour of the Channel and its snaking coasts to the north and east, and the elegant ridges of Quantock to the south and west this is a memorable spot. We left the road and took the footpath to Kilton, then a short stretch of uphill road before heading off along the ridge on sticky, yellow clay. The views were still magnificent but the going underfoot was grim on this slippery stuff, the ground here littered with stones and planted with brassica, presumably the ubiquitous oil-seed rape. We left the open fields and entered Waltham's Copse, an intriguing, boggy, oak woodland with a few scattered hazels and a dense ground-cover of stinking iris. The oaks appear to be all much the same age, I would guess about fifty years old, and this and their lay-out strongly suggest they were planted, perhaps for the benefit of pheasants, rather than being the remnant of a natural woodland. Roxie sloped off to investigate in approved Longdog fashion but found nothing of interest. At the edge of the wood we found some Spindleberry, with its shocking-pink fruits, and a tangle of Crosswort, both indicators of the limey soil now stuck to our boots. We trudged across the slippery, stony fields with the light fading behind a bluish quarter-moon and the bright eye of Venus sharp against the pastel sky. The wind dropped to stillness and we walked on in a soft, velvet blanket of silence.

Another short stretch of road took us through the hamlet of Burton where we turned off onto an easy, grassy path across gently sloping fields towards the towering light-show of Hinkley Point backed by the spangling Welsh coast across the water. I have never seen the Blackpool illuminations, but it is hard to imagine that they could exceed this nuclear-powered blaze of glory.

We crossed a bridleway and met The Fence. In the gloom we could just read the notice on the wire: "No Unauthorised Access. Protected Site Under Section 128 of the Serious Organised Crime and Police Act 2005." Crikey! The security guards' pick-up was still lurking on the ridge so we ducked behind a hedge and kept out of sight as the truck started up and moved down towards us. We kept under cover as we headed back towards the road, adding a bit of interest, we hoped, to what must have been a pretty dull shift for those guards. We found a gap in the hedge and slid out onto the road, remaining undetected and missing out the odd meanderings of the fence we had encountered at the beginning.

The car was still there, safe under the watchful eye of the cameras which, no doubt, had logged our number somewhere in the grumbling bowels of this grim edifice. As we drove away we reflected on the day which, with all its interesting snippets and magnificent vistas, we had to admit was dominated by the power station and its almost endless fence. It would be interesting to know the reasoning which led to this remarkable place being chosen for such a monstrous installation. Wouldn't somewhere along the Thames have been more appropriate?

Kilve to Blue Anchor

With Chris and Lottie

Leaving the car in the Kilve village car-park we strolled about a mile down Sea Lane and back to the beach. The sun shone and the stiff breeze ruffled Roxie's coat as we climbed the path to the cliff top overlooking the famous lias pavements running down to the receding silvery sea. The coast of Wales was a mirage-blur in the haze across the water to the north on this bright and beautiful winter's day.

Inland, the sun sitting on top of the Quantocks picked out the prominent bulk of the Court House at East Quantoxhead, the only building visible from here. (I have no explanation for the use of the 'x' in Quantoxhead, but there it is on the map, so it must be right.) The Court House doesn't really look much like Hinkley Point, but its fortified facade is similarly menacing. It occupies the site of a manor given by William the Conqueror to one of his henchmen in 1086, presumably replacing its original Saxon occupants. The estate was acquired by the Luttrell family in 1229 and has remained in their descendants' hands ever since. One of the most notable of its many and various incumbents must be Lady Silvestra Skory (d.1655), a Luttrell widow, whose tyrannical behaviour included throwing her hapless second husband out of a window. As Sir Edmund lived for a few years after the event we can assume it was from one of the lower stories, but one is bound to wonder as to the fate of her first husband.

The imposing pile we can now see was built in the early 17th century and became known as the Court House around 1865 when local sessions were held there following the decline of the church house, the former seat of law and order. Looking at the rather stern frontage today, even from a safe distance, it is not difficult to imagine the deployment of the pillory and cucking-stool on this site in ages past.

Turning our backs on the feudal savageries of relatively recent history we continued along the slippery cliff-top path towards the promontory of Quantocks Head (no 'x' this time) to encounter again the geological past. A long flight of steep metal steps leads down to the beach where the receding tide was revealing more of the spectacular fossil-bearing pavements curving seawards. The stratum we were standing on was deposited around 200 million years ago, and we know that somewhere here is the Global Boundary Stratotype Section and Point which marks the internationally-recognised transition between the two parts of the Lower Lias succession 196.5 million years ago. This is of great significance to geologists but, alas, we couldn't find it, so we headed off west along the rocky beach.

The going underfoot was tricky: the rocks are of all shapes and sizes and many were inconveniently coated with slippery algae. Even Roxie proceeded with caution, looking strangely like a giant, dainty mouse as she picked her way over the treacherous stones. The limestone pavements, dipping at an angle of about 30°, were equally slippery, so we tried walking on the swathes of brown seaweeds which proved to be slightly less hazardous. We squelched on with care, distracted only by a glorious peregrine which detached itself from the cliff, taking a close look at us before cruising off to the east. Occasional patches of bare sand came as a welcome relief from the slippery scrambling, so we followed them seaward and put a bit of distance between us and the prospect of descending rocks, many of which litter the beach under the unstable cliff.

On this stretch of coast, we know there are fossils in profusion, but it is still a delight to find well-preserved ammonites, some up to 60cm across, and countless bivalves packed together in the rock, one unusual specimen about 12cm long. We had no geological hammer but, if we had, I confess I might well have been tempted. As we approached the next promontory, called Blue Ben on the map, the strata in the cliffs are folded and faulted in staggering patterns. We struggled to imagine just how these rocks, even in a more plastic state, could have acquired these amazing shapes from their original horizontal layers. Still marvelling, we rounded Blue Ben to find a huge fault separating the blue lias from beds of red Keuper marls. The idea of the power and scale of the forces responsible for these massive shifts is almost beyond imagination.

We moved gratefully off the rocks onto a huge expanse of sand and strode out comfortably for the first time since descending the steps at Quantock's Head. Up ahead we could see the first people we had encountered so far, including a charming lady and her small daughter flying a kite and accompanied by a lively Saluki lurcher. Roxie took off like a rocket, and the pair raced around in huge circles, sand flying in all directions in an explosion of canine joie de vivre. Just watching their pace and grace was exhilarating. Perhaps unwisely, Chris released the ill-tempered Lottie, resulting in a noisy three-dog brawl which might well have ended in bloodshed had we not intervened with some determination. The lady was quite unperturbed as I untangled Roxie from the kite strings and, with the disgraced Lottie once more securely leashed, the two elegant hounds resumed their high-speed manoeuvres.

Rather reluctantly, I confess, we left the Lady of the Lurcher and pressed on across the sand towards a dramatic waterfall cascading out of the next headland. Alongside it a flight of steps descends to the beach from a 'Holiday Village', the roofs of which were just visible along the cliff-top. This stretch of the coast is dotted with these sometimes huge collections of the wonderfully oxymoronic 'static mobile homes', these providing the bulk of the holiday accommodation on which this area sadly depends. As we marvelled at the waterfall tumbling over the multi-coloured rocks, our second peregrine of the day glided past, its hapless prey clutched in unyielding talons.

The cliffs begin to slope down as we moved on towards Watchet, the soft, crumbling faces protected by defences of huge boulders. We were picking our way cautiously over an expanse of irregular, broken rocks with Watchet, and lunch, not far ahead, when our course was obstructed by The Swill, the broad, fast-moving outlet of a small but significant river flanked by a huge concrete pipe running out to sea. Thwarted, we took the only option and struck inland through another deserted holiday park, where the only sign of life was a brace of JCB's busily clearing more ground, presumably for expansion. In the summer season this place is alive with holidaymakers, many with the oingy-boingy twang of the Midlands or the sing-song cadences of south Wales, and we acknowledged gratefully how lucky we are to live in Somerset all year round while these short-term visitors are blessed with only a week or two.

Sneaking through what seemed like hundreds of empty, identical 'statics' we were delighted by the notices attached to almost every one: "This Unit Has Been Closed Down for the Winter and Contains No Valuables." We wondered about the few which were lacking this off-putting declaration: Could they be stuffed full of all the valuable booty? We resisted the temptation to investigate and escaped through the unmanned security barrier at the entrance and onto the road.

We crossed The Swill over a small, stone bridge and followed the road a short distance through Doniford with only moderate risk to life from the occasional vehicle. There is an air of rather bleak emptiness about Doniford at this time of year, so we were glad to turn off the road and return to the beach by way of an unobtrusive little car park set in what must have been a small quarry, complete with its own lime-kiln. Burning limestone to produce mortar and agricultural lime was common practice in many parts of the county, and the remains of the kilns are widespread. Many of them are impressive structures, and this one at Doniford would pass for the ruin of a small temple.

We descended the steps and regained the beach, which is not as well-known as Kilve and is none the worse for that. Between the bottom of these steps and The Swill to the east I have often found fossils of the bivalve mollusc known as Devil's Toenails. If you are lucky enough to find one of these curved, black shells, about two or three centimetres long, you will see how they earn their name. Resisting the temptation to hunt for toenails we turned west and headed for Watchet along a stony beach towards Helwell Bay, where the loose, crumbly cliffs are much lower, and necessarily protected by more of the huge boulder defences. Ahead, the big, red cliffs guarding the east side of Watchet harbour rear up, and after crossing the sandy expanse of the bay we climbed a long flight of steps to a strip of grassy, brambly wasteland at the top. The West Somerset Railway track sits in a cutting to our left, and we followed the footpath beside it before descending more steps leading down to Watchet marina.

In contrast to the wildness of the shore and cliffs, the marina has the look of a pretty postcard with a flotilla of leisure craft resting on the low water. It was not always so. Perhaps its most notable historical event took place in the Civil War, in 1643, when the bold Captain Popham led a cavalry charge into the sea to capture a Royalist ship which had intended to land a force to relieve the siege of Dunster Castle. This is the only action in naval history in which a ship technically 'at sea' was taken by cavalry.

The old harbour was in use from pre-Saxon times, its original wooden construction wrecked by the sea and rebuilt on numerous occasions over the centuries. Even the sturdier stone-built version was sea-broken in 1900 and at least three times since, but the proud port of Watchet has always bounced back. Once rightly known as a nest of smugglers, the port has also enjoyed much legitimate business including importing coal and timber, and exporting lime, wool, hides and iron from the Brendon Hills, but by the 1960's trade had declined drastically. Fortunately, in 2001, the very smart marina was opened, and this has brought a new lease of life to this charming little town.

We stopped for lunch on one of the seats along the tastefully-appointed quay. Passers-by included strolling locals and out-of-season holidaymakers (you need not be an anthropologist to tell the difference), some pausing to admire the elegantly sprawled Roxie, who received their attention with her customary supercilious dignity.

With some reluctance we left the quayside and walked the short distance past the museum (unfortunately closed today), stoically resisted the temptation of Pebbles Tavern with its exceptional range of ciders (and admirably run by one of my ex-students,) and passed down the slipway onto the rocky beach. The loose, red cliffs are marbled with multi-coloured bands of gypsum from dried-up Triassic seas and these, with the dramatic faulting and folding of the strata, make this a seriously impressive bit of geology. Many of the rocks scattered about the beach are full of countless bivalve shells and, here and there, exquisite small, iridescent ammonites.

Looking out to the still-retreating tide we could see more of the rows of posts we first saw way back at Lilstock. Here, there were nets strung between the posts, showing that mud-fishing is not entirely dead hereabouts, though we guess that these are too close inshore to require the famous Stolford mud-horse. We set out across the expanse of mud and sand that will take us to Blue Anchor. Even though we were still close to the fabulously stratified cliffs, the great sweep of the bay reflecting the lowering sunlight gave a feeling of immense airy space. The beach was dotted with people and dogs in the distance but, after the exercise with the saluki, Roxie was content to lope along beside us and leave the ball-chasers in peace. We climbed the slipway up onto the Blue Anchor promenade, stretching ahead for almost a mile in a graceful, sweeping curve of geometric concrete. The low-lying fields and caravan parks on the landward side of the road are way below us, and the need for the monumental sea defences is clear. As clouds began to pile up from the south-west we met my daughter who kindly provided the taxi service back to Kilve, where the Hood Arms awaited.

Blue Anchor to Minehead

With Chris & Lottie

We started where we left off at the west end of Blue Anchor's sweeping promenade, this time on a pale grey morning with the grey sea chopped into breakers by a cutting wind. There is a claim that Blue Anchor is the only Somerset village to be named after a pub but, as the said hostelry is a mile away at the other end of the prom that seems less than likely. Alternative explanations include reference to the distinctive blue woollen cloth made in Watchet in the 16th century, perhaps dyed with local wortleberries, (and reputed to be the lining of Charles I's cloak when he parted company with his head) or from the blue colouring of some of the alabaster found in the local rocks. They all sound like nonsense to me but, either way, one has to be careful with the pronunciation.

Ancient, blackened timber breakwater posts snaggle above the rising tide like spiky, rotten teeth. These one-time coastal defences are marked on the map as 'Ker Moor pilings' and their position about 30 yards down the shore from the present high-tide mark shows the extent of erosion since they were planted, probably in the 19th century. Heads down, we butted into the wind along the pebble bank separating the beach from the flat fields inland, Roxie picking her way over the knobbly, pebbly path with obvious resentment.

Beyond the fields we could see the almost-conical wooded hump of Conygar Hill fronting the steep, dark shoulders of Exmoor beyond. The hill is topped with a stone-built tower completed in 1775 at the behest of yet another Luttrell. Contemporary accounts describe it as "designed to impress" and "built to improve the view from Dunster Castle", while others suggest that it was intended as a landmark for shipping. The latter seems unlikely, as the little harbour at the mouth of the River Avill was silted up in the 17th century so 'the folly', as it is known locally, describes it appropriately enough. At a total cost of seventy-six pounds and eleven shillings, of which four pounds two shillings and sixpence was spent on cider for the workmen, it must have seemed like a bargain for three years work.

Moving on, we came to a small wooden bridge crossing the mouth of the same R. Avill, and the majesty of Dunster Castle itself became clearly visible. Now here is some real history. The site has been occupied since Bronze Age times and perhaps before, but was first seriously fortified by the Anglo-Saxons, probably against Viking raiders. The last Saxon incumbent was the gallant Aelfric who died alongside Harold at Hastings. After the Norman Conquest it was given, along with sixty-eight other manors, to William de Mohun, who reinforced the fortress as "part of the pacification of Somerset" in the bloody and regrettably unsuccessful anti-Norman rebellion of 1068. Further fortifications were added by a succession of Mohuns, particularly by the third William, known as "the scourge of the West" and a nasty piece of work by all accounts. He was involved in 'The Anarchy' (1135-1153) when various factions of the Nasty Normans fought it out for the throne, mostly with the help of mercenaries and other bad lots. Hard times, indeed, for Somerset.

In 1376, or thereabouts, the Mohuns finally petered out and the Castle was sold to the Luttrells (more Normans), from nearby East Quantoxhead, who have been responsible, over the generations, for most of the building as it is today. The Castle took a bit of a battering in the Civil War, in which its inmates seemed to have had some difficulty in deciding which side to be on but, thereafter, settled down to become a grand country house rather than a fort. The Luttrells finally handed over to the National Trust in 1976 after around 600 years of more or less continuous occupation. It must be said that from here, on the coast, the Castle as it is today looks like something out of a fairy tale.

Coming back to reality, we emerged onto the east end of Dunster Beach with the tide receding. Taking to the exposed sand, Roxie celebrated her liberation from the tiresome pebbles with a long, looping gallop and, spotting a couple of collies in the middle distance, she launched into one of her usual playful assaults, rolling over one of the hapless piebalds with her speciality high-speed nudge. Unfortunately, the delinquent Lottie, close behind, pounced on the tumbling collie with obvious intent toward a spot of GBH. The other collie and Roxie joined in the ensuing brawl, just for the fun of it, and we were forced to intervene again, hauling off the aggressors and apologising profusely to the somewhat disconcerted collie people. (If that Lottie were mine ....!) In disgrace, we retreated to the upper level of the beach and sheltered behind one of the new timber groynes for a coffee break.

On the landward side of the pebble bank, a double row of well-kept, more or less identical wooden chalets stood deserted. (This was January, after all.) Whilst the chalets lack the antiquity of Dunster Castle they are equally reminiscent of a bygone age; in the case of the chalets I should think the 1950's. There must be at least two hundred of them, and we can only wonder what it must be like here at the height of the summer season, and who the inhabitants might be. Behind the beach huts lies The Hawn, which appears on the map as a long, narrow stretch of water running parallel to the beach. This is all that remains of the Haven, or sheltered harbour, which linked with the R. Avill to provide water transport to Dunster before silting up in the 17th century. Despite the map's assertion, the water is now barely visible, being overgrown with reedbeds at the east end and trees to the west, but still providing a variety of habitats as part of the local nature reserve.

With the collies out of sight and Lottie firmly on the leash we set out along the beach towards Minehead. Pebbles soon took over from the sand so we climbed back onto the bank and looked down on a gathering of waders along the tide line. A couple of hundred Dunlin along with a scattering of Turnstone and Ringed Plover huddled among the rocks, while a delightful trio of almost-white Sanderling scampered up and down a bit of exposed sand like clockwork mice, chasing the waves. A raft of a hundred or so Widgeon were sitting it out just offshore and a flock of fifty Curlew tumbled in from landward and pitched down among a bunch of piebald Oystercatchers. 'Real' bird-watchers would surely have set up their huge telescopes at this point, and meticulously 'gone through' the flocks to identify any rarities, but we only admired them and moved on, leaving any oddities in peace.

In contrast to the wild shore, inland from our viewpoint lay a golf course, with a scattering of multi-coloured participants in odd hats swiping rather ineptly at their little white balls. From here it is not readily apparent what they are trying to do, or why, but they make an eye-catching spectacle nonetheless. Beyond them, the monstrous white pimples of Butlin's holiday camp loomed large. After a period of relative doldrums when it was renamed Somerwest World, old Billy's outfit seems to have regained its popularity, and was swarming with people even in January. God only knows what they're all doing here and, given that the place is popular for religious Conventions, that may well be the case.

As we hit the sweeping, wind-blown sands of Minehead beach, the sun came out and we looked ahead along the seaward side of the curving promenade to the picturesque west end of the town, with the tacky sea-front shops and arcades blessedly out of sight above the sea wall. The old harbour on the point, the handsome Georgian and Victorian buildings and the steep dignity of West Hill give a real sense of the town's former glory, surely a delightful watering-hole in the 'good old days'.

Back to the present, and lunch-time was calling. An excellent fish-and-chip stall provided the necessary, and we dodged the wind in a pleasantly old-fashioned sea-front shelter, Roxie and Lottie receiving their share as of right. Hounds of their ilk will eat anything, as long as it was originally intended for human consumption or is in an advanced state of decomposition. The sun disappeared as quickly as it had arrived and rain moved in from the west with a vengeance, driving the promenade strollers to run for cover. Enquiries revealed that there is only one dog-friendly pub in Minehead, so we set off at speed for the shelter of the aptly-named Hairy Dog, which is otherwise remarkable on account of its size, the vast number of trees which must have been slain to furnish its interior and the staggering array of television screens simultaneously showing a variety of sports. Good cider is rarely to be found in this kind of pub, but the Exmoor ale was an acceptable substitute. Roxie prowled majestically around, befriending the ladies and basking in the admiration and attention, perhaps bearing out my daughter's view that she is the best 'pull' in the book, whatever that means. With beer and rain finished for the time being, we made our way down Minehead's main street. Had we been in need of a tattoo, a bucket and spade, a coffee or some outlandish seaside clothing we would have been in the right place, even in January. Otherwise not.

A surprisingly convenient bus transported us to Carhampton, from where we trudged across flat, rain-swept fields back to our starting-point at Blue Anchor. From the veranda of the excellent, dog-friendly Driftwood Café we looked out over the pale, rain-washed sweep of the bay before strolling the last few yards back to the car at the end of another fascinating and varied Somerset border day.

Minehead to Porlock Weir

With Miranda

Towards the western end of the Minehead promenade there stands an enormous structure (sculpture?) marking the official beginning of the South West Coast Path. The pair of giant hands holding what we took to be a map towered over us, and I paused to wonder what possessed the 'authorities', whoever they may be, to erect such an edifice. Only slightly intimidated by this mini-mountain of metal, we scuttled off in search of a pre-walk coffee. We first investigated the Old Ship Aground, an imposing hostelry set on the quayside of the picturesque old harbour but, alas, the Old Ship appeared to be the Marie Celeste this morning as, despite the doors being open giving ready access to the interior, we could find no sign of life on board. Thankfully, we did find a nearby dog-friendly café which provided the necessary stimulants before we embarked on our ascent through the woods which border the north western end of the town.

Considering that this is part of a National Trail, no less, the way-marking is poor here at the beginning of the Coast Path, and the distinctive logo of an acorn (or coconut for the more imaginative or whimsical) is difficult to find. In fact, we were unable to find it at all so, with the dubious assistance of the map, we headed up steeply through the woods past hefty sandstone outcrops among big conifers and holm oaks. The beach seemed like a long way below already, and the receding tide, still close in, was tempting a few gallant rod fishermen to keep their futile vigil along the water's edge. We continued to climb and, with no sign of the acorns/coconuts, we trusted the map again and turned back on ourselves up another steep slope. After a further hairpin our path followed the contour westward, and we emerged eventually from the wood into the open heathland and cropped grass where, at last, we found our first genuine Coast Path way-marker. Following the path inland we gained more height as the ground dropped away to the north with gathering speed to the cliff tops, with steep-sided combes slicing down to the sea some 200m below. To the south the bulk of Exmoor, gloriously wooded on this side, rose to a dramatic skyline, with Dunkery Beacon looking almost mountainous in the distance.

Sticking to the now well-marked Coast Path, at this point half a mile of sheep-dotted fields from the coast itself, we passed close to Selworthy Beacon (308m) and looked inland towards the delightful little town of Porlock. From here it could hardly be prettier or more peaceful, neatly tucked into the bottom of heavily wooded combes but, like so many Somerset settlements, there is no shortage of violence and bloodshed in its history. As well as repelling the occasional Viking raid, ancient Porlock was the seat of a succession of Saxon kings whose internecine brawling was characteristic of the pre-Norman age. In 1052, for example, Harold Godwinson, later to become King Harold of arrow-in-the-eye fame, returned from exile in Ireland and ravaged Porlock before rampaging across Somerset on his way to a distinguished political and military career which terminated abruptly in 1066.

We stopped for lunch on the headland overlooking Hurlstone Point, a glorious spot, with the jagged rocks of the Point tapering down to the sea far below. To the west the great sweep of Porlock Bay, bordered by a curving pebble bank, reaches round to the promontory of Gore Point just beyond Porlock Weir, which was our destination for the day. Cruising gulls and wind-tossed corvids added to the wildness of this dramatic seascape.

We were now facing the descent from the top of Bossington Hill down Hurlstone Combe to return to sea level. The path is not only seriously steep and muddy but had been carved up by the tyre tracks of a couple of lunatics who must have descended on mountain bikes. I award them points for their courage (or commiserations for their insanity), but the effect on the surface was less than helpful. I found myself sliding from one side to the other before losing my footing altogether and rolling down the slope in a far from elegant fashion. From the far end of a long lead Roxie observed the performance with detached interest, and casually ambled over to assess the damage while Miranda, with commendable compassion, refrained from laughing out loud. None the worse for the tumble, we carried on down the hill as a perky male Stonechat looked on, entirely at home hopping about on the broad swathe of scree on the north-east slope of the steep-sided combe.

The last leg of the descent took us on an angle across the slope through a handsome deciduous wood to a burbling stream at the bottom. Crossing the bridge which leads to the pretty car-park on the seaward side of Bossington we met another lurcher and, while the dogs exchanged more or less amiable greetings, his companion and I exchanged the usual lurcher tales of woe: disappearances, disobedience, injuries, fights, vets' bills, cat 'incidents' etc., and agreed that they are undoubtedly the finest dogs on Earth.

From the car-park (complete with convenient conveniences) our path followed a minimal road down to the beach. I remember clearly coming across a field of fine mangel-wurzels down here a few years ago but, alas, could see no sign of them today. My companion seemed somewhat bemused by my nostalgic affection for this magnificent fodder-crop but then, she is not a native of Somerset so may be forgiven for lacking an appreciation of this king of roots.

Reaching the end of the road we climbed the significant pebble bank which is Bossington Beach, to be greeted by the roars and groans of the tide shifting and heaving through the Somerset version of Chesil Bank. Roxie is never happy on pebbles, and these were no exception. In a range of pinks and greys and varying in size from hens'- to ostrich-eggs they make awkward walking for humans too, so we descended the landward side of the bank onto the boggy scrub bordering Porlock Marsh. While we could barely hear the sea from here it was obvious that the recent high tides had been over the pebble bank leaving scattered flotsam and an uncomfortably squelchy surface.

Exactly where we diverged from the official Coast Path is still not clear, but we found ourselves continuing along the landward side of the shingle while the map shows the Coast Path cutting inland around the low-lying bog which is Porlock Marsh. Once again the acorn/coconut way-marking eluded us. As the afternoon light began to fade we watched Shelduck, Little Egrets and Curlews feeding along the ditches across the marsh, the calls of the latter lending a rather mournful air to this soggy stretch. The Marsh is now a designated Site of Special Scientific Interest (SSSI) since it became a salt-marsh when the shingle bank was breached by exceptionally fierce high tides in the 1990's. Rather than attempting to repair the damage, the Powers That Be decided to allow the incursions to continue, so the distinctive and rare salt-marsh communities are maintained, thus earning the SSSI status.

As the haven of Porlock Weir came into welcome view up ahead we discovered the breach in the sea-defences at first hand. We were confronted by a pebble-free stretch of hard, yellow clay divided by a wide, but thankfully shallow, pebble-bedded river rushing out to sea to meet the incoming tide. This was The Breach. Having negotiated the wickedly slippery clay we had no choice but to cross this shallow torrent, Roxie leading the way with slightly sullen resignation. The water was a little deeper than anticipated and the pebbles a little slippier, so I ended up with boots full of water for only the second time on this trek, but the sensation was quite pleasant once the water had warmed up.

Our heroic river crossing was ill-rewarded. We were faced with almost half a mile of unavoidable pebble bank which, surely, can't be the actual Coast Path route which, according to the map, we should have rejoined about here. None of us was overjoyed by this pebbly stuff but we pressed on gallantly until the pebble-scrambling terminated in an escape route up a short flight of steps onto the road a couple of hundred yards short of Porlock Weir. The cottages on the seaward side of the road are almost impossibly picturesque, but our attention was focussed on the equally pretty and even more attractive Bottom Ship Inn. (This handsome hostelry earns its unusual name, it seems, in deference to the Top Ship Inn which is in Porlock itself, a mile or so to the east, and certainly a contour or two higher.) Our anticipation of the delights of the inn was cruelly extended by the need to check the timetable on the bus-stop opposite to see if we could get back to Minehead today. Intense perusal informed us that the next bus would arrive in forty minutes time. Perfect!

I have said before that a dog-friendly pub is generally a good one, and this is no exception. There must have been at least half a dozen assorted canines in the bar, including a labrador puppy with which Roxie seemed quite happy to share the adoration of the assembled company. After an excellent pint of Exmoor Ale, we made our way back across the road to the bus-stop where we met another pair of walkers recently disgorged from the pub having completed the first stage of their South West Coast Path walk. We wished each other well in our respective adventures as we climbed aboard the bus.

The lady bus driver handled her substantial chariot as if it were a Mini Cooper, which made for an exhilarating ride along the side-scraping lane out of Porlock Weir, through the narrow, cluttered streets of Porlock and along the bendy A39 to Minehead. Safely

disembarked and glad to be alive, we found the high tide slapping
the sea wall and the low sun putting metallic highlights on the waves
as we strolled back along the promenade to the car-park. Another
delightful end to another delightful day along the penultimate
coastal stretch of Somerset's border.

Porlock Weir to County Gate

With Chris

Porlock Weir on a pale, misty morning with the promise of a fine day to come. The tide was in, and small boats were bobbing about on an almost-blue, side-slapping sea as we made our way along what was once the quay. The old quayside buildings are now cafés and craft workshops with the Harbour Stores and a boat museum thrown in, but it is still a very pretty place.

We climbed a short flight of steep steps and took the path parallel to the coast along the bottom of a couple of sheep-filled fields, with the sea sparkling hazily to our right and the wooded flank of Exmoor rising steeply to our left. At the end of the fields we hit a short stretch of tarmac road leading to the arched entrance of the Worthy toll-road. This is not to be confused with the Porlock toll-road (or New Road) which was built in the 1840's as an alternative to the notoriously steep Porlock Hill which is the main road to Lynmouth and beyond. The history of the Worthy version is obscure, but must be something to do with the Ashley Combe Estate which flourished briefly in the middle of the 19th century when Ashley Combe House was rebuilt for the delectation of the Countess Lovelace (neé Ada Byron, daughter of Lord Byron) when she married the multi-titled William King in 1835. Old pictures of the place show it to be a classic example of the lunatic extravagance of the time, with turrets, towers and countless windows. The house has long since been demolished and the estate has sunk to the level of a private pheasant shoot but, as we began the climb across the wooded hillside, we encountered further evidence of Ada's activities: At several points the path passes through short stone tunnels or extended arches. The original purpose of these is not clear, but it seems likely that they were components of Ada's elaborate garden or, as we might call them today, follies. (It would be unfair to dismiss Ada Lovelace as just another barmy folly-maker, as she was a notable mathematician and, perhaps, the first computer programmer, remarkable achievements for a lady of that time.)

The path took us up through the woods and across the hillside rising to about 200m above the sea before we dropped down into the steep combe harbouring the delightful Culbone Church, which claims to be the smallest parish church in England and certainly has an air of Lilliput about it. This is an ancient and wonderful spot. The church is probably of Saxon origin, or possibly earlier, but the present building was reconstructed in the 12th century and has been lovingly maintained and occasionally modified through the ages since. An instructive leaflet in the porch informed us that in 1280 Thomas, the chaplain, was indicted ..."for that he had struck Albert Esshe on the head with a hatchet and so killed him." The fate of the homicidal parson is not recorded, but the leaflet assures us that "this kind of incident does not now take place in our tiny parish." Comforted by this assurance, we sat on the conveniently-placed seat in the churchyard for a coffee break while Roxie optimistically investigated the assembled gravestones. These are dominated by the families Richards and Red, mostly from the 19th century but including some more recent residents. So many intriguing stories of old Somerset must lie in these beautiful little country churchyards.

Leaving the church, we re-joined the path past the old mill, now apparently a residence, and opted for the Permissive path running along the top of steep, wooded slopes dropping to the cliff-tops below. A tumble from here would result in a pin-ball descent through the stunted oaks followed by a terminal drop onto the rocky beach, so Roxie patiently submitted to the lead, perhaps acknowledging that any hunting sorties from here could well be her last. As the path took us down steep, fairy-tale combes with waterfall streams and stepping-stone crossings the sun finally shrugged off its misty cloak, dappling through the trees while the sea-sound washed up from far below. If Paradise is anything like this I hereby resolve to be exceptionally good in future.

We stopped for lunch sitting on huge boulders at the top of a precipitous drop overlooking a pebble beach down below. A family of walkers approached from the west, and a small boy came over and asked, hopefully, "Le chien, c'est gentile?" (Her head is level with his shoulder.) "Oui, *tres* gentile," I assured him, and the little lad happily stroked her head before trotting off to re-join his family. Another group came close behind. This time I only caught the word 'hund' from a handsome blonde woman, but I can recognise admiration when I hear it in any language so I managed, "Ja, danke," the only words of German I know, and everyone smiled, in a kindly if slightly superior sort of way. Over the pebble beach way down below a peregrine passed backwards and forwards, perhaps on hunting sorties to provide for his mate on the cliffs.

Suitably refreshed, and cheered by our international encounters, we pressed on and, after crossing another delightful and precipitous water-fall combe, we re-joined the 'official' Coast Path for a short stretch before opting for a steep (steep!) downhill track signposted Glenthorne Beach, which marks the border with Devon.

A further descent took us through the remarkable Halliday's Pinetum, established by the Rev. W. S. Halliday in the mid-19th century and now a nature reserve. The many and various huge, specimen conifers dotted around the slopes bear testament to the reverend gentleman's botanical enthusiasm. The reserve is now the home of rare butterflies but, alas, we are too early in the year to see them. We followed the stream which marks the border down to the beach itself, a pebbly inlet flanked by crumbly red cliffs. A pair of Fulmars, a bit of a rarity in Somerset, were cruising around on characteristically stiff wings, but our attention was drawn to the extensive stone buildings which stand against the bottom of the cliff and at the top of a short slip-way. Our investigation revealed an enormous double lime-kiln plus a couple of barn-like structures with entrances big enough to suggest boat-houses. The lime-burning activities here probably began as early as the 15th century and continued until the 19th, both raw materials and products presumably being transported to and from by sea, via the adjacent slip-way. The idea of *walking* back up the path we had recently descended is daunting enough, but the prospect of hauling coal, stone or lime either way, even with the most willing of horses, makes the sea a more likely option.

Roxie had regarded the pebbly beach with mournful anticipation but perked up when we turned our backs on the sea and commenced the climb back up the border line. We noted, with a little trepidation, that for the first time we were actually on what is now the Devon side, but an incongruous llama peering at us from the paddock of a huge, seemingly 'modernised' house to the west seemed to bear us no ill will. As we continued to climb we noticed sign-posts indicating a former ice-house and trout-breeding pond, both evidence of the former glory hereabouts. This was the stiffest climb yet, and we had to admit to puffing a bit when we decided on a detour enticingly signposted as Sisters Fountain. The track entered the typical sterile gloom of a monoculture conifer plantation (I wonder what the Rev. Halliday would think of this lot?) but soon emerged into an area of more open mixed woodland. Looking downhill we could see what we assumed to be the 'fountain', which appears as a small stone cairn with a hefty cross on top. This is yet another 19th century whimsy concerning the journey of Joseph of Arimethea from Judea through the West Country to Glastonbury accompanied, according to some scholars, by the young Jesus. Having stopped off to replenish his ship's water supply, Joseph seems to have missed the stream running down to Glenthorne beach and searched for a spring on this hillside. Failing to find one he struck the ground with his famous staff and lo! Water sprang forth. (This self-same staff doubtless went on to become the progenitor of the famous Glastonbury Thorn.)

Turning south we faced a steep climb through open grassland up to Black Gate on the A39. We climbed about 340m (1100ft) in half a mile, so it's no wonder that we were puffing a bit. A short stroll alongside the road eastwards brought us back to the border at County Gate, which is marked by a car-park, toilets and a café-cum-information centre. We arrived just before four o'clock, and my internet bus timetable had assured me that a bus for Porlock would be here at 4.15. (Do I never learn? See the Brean Down bus saga.) The timetable in the bus-shelter, alas, had expired in February (it's now April) so I ventured into the 'information' centre/shop/café to seek, yes, information. It is not my habit to criticise the afflicted, but the old chap in sole charge of the whole outfit was, shall we say, unskilled in public relations, a bit light on information and less than helpful. In response to my question re. the bus timetable he informed me, in very few words and entirely without expression, that he didn't know (anything) because, "I'm not from round here." My slightly ironic "Thank you very much", was entirely lost on the Zombie, so I shuffled out to break the news to Chris and Roxie that we might be in for a further, six-mile walk back to Porlock.

Some other bus-anticipators we found in the car-park were more optimistic, expecting, they told us, a bus from Porlock to Lynmouth at 4.50. This is in the opposite direction from the one we required, of course, but if the same bus should then turn around and return to Porlock (possible if not likely) then we would be in luck - assuming it existed at all. This was, after all, a Bank Holiday Saturday so, in customary West Country fashion, the services would be reduced at best or abandoned altogether.

At five o'clock the fabled bus to Lynmouth arrived and I beseechingly asked the jolly driver if there was any chance of a bus going to Porlock in the foreseeable future and, joy of joys, he replied in the affirmative. "When?" I asked, plaintively. "As long as it takes me to turn this bugger round and come back," he said cheerfully, and roared off towards Lynmouth. We guessed about half an hour, but any hopes of tea and cakes from the café were promptly dashed by the Zombie shutting up shop as we approached the door. Murder is not in my nature but .... Instead, we hunkered down at the roadside out of the wind and waited. Within our estimated thirty minutes we were on the bus and negotiating the formidable bends and gradients of Porlock Hill as we descended once again to sea level.

After disembarking in Porlock we strolled along a mile or so of quiet road back to Porlock Weir, enjoying a beautiful, balmy spring evening in a truly lovely setting with the sea sparkling on one side and the mighty green flanks of Exmoor on the other. The blissful tranquillity was only disturbed when Roxie spotted a roadside cat which had clearly never encountered a felicidal hound before. The wretched thing simply stood there looking bemused while the usually saintly Roxie went berserk on the end of the lead, attempting to remove my arms from their sockets. The satanic angels which protect cats must have been out in force as I resisted the obvious temptation and steered her back on course despite her vociferous protests.

And so to the Bottom Ship once again. This was a brilliant day, perhaps the best yet, and another pint of Exmoor Ale was a fitting finale.

Interlude 2

Somerset Dogs

Dogs are man's best friend and all that, wherever they are but, allowing for a certain amount of natural prejudice on my part, Somerset air seems to bring out the best in them. Let me offer you a few notable examples.

Bramble. Some years ago, my younger daughter decided it would be A Good Thing to adopt a dog. Having gained the acquiescence of her long-suffering husband and being about as rational in these matters as I am, she reckoned a retired greyhound would be just the thing. Bramble (aka Bramley Arrow) was duly acquired from an Oxfordshire racing kennel and, when eventually brought home to Somerset, soon became the amiable, bone-idle, potentially lethal prima donna (can you have a male prima donna?) you would expect a retired track-star to be.

Other than stealing any food within reach - which was plenty, as he had the reach of a giraffe - he was the perfect sofa-lounging, enormous lap-dog when at home. When out and about, however, his canine inner self emerged. Anything smallish and furryish became the 'hare' of his glory days so, after a couple of slightly embarrassing incidents, my daughter was obliged to keep him on the lead.   As she is of a particularly compassionate nature she also insisted that he wore a light muzzle when in public, "just in case".

I'm no fan of muzzles so, when they were staying with me and I took Bramble and my own dog, George, out for an early morning stroll, I ignored the shrieked "Don't forget the muzzle!" as I made a hasty exit.

As we returned up the lane after an unsuccessful rabbiting sortie I noticed a stranger coming towards us, complete with a baby in a pushchair and a terrier on a lead. Holding both Bramble and George by their collars I stood aside to let the stranger pass. As he did so, Bramble slipped backwards out of his collar, leapt clean over the pushchair and grabbed the terrier as he would have snaffled the 'hare' in his racing days. As the terrified terrier owner jumped up and down and howled, I dived onto the triumphant hound and prized the squeaking terrier from his jaws. No mean feat.

The unfortunate victim took off back up the lane whence he'd come, hotly pursued by the pushchair and its driver while I was left wrestling with a collarless, squirming greyhound. Within seconds he'd wriggled free and, in a few lightning bounds, caught the poor terrier again and held it aloft in renewed triumph. Fortunately, he made no attempt to damage it further; he just held it in his alligator jaws and looked pleased.

I pounced again and repeated the terrier extraction. This time I was left flat on my back in the road clutching the slippery hound to my chest while the pushchair and company retreated at even greater speed without a backward glance. The poor chap must have thought that this form of terrier-bating was some barbaric local custom.

I was in a bit of a fix. I daren't release my grip or try to get up for fear of unleashing the hell-hound yet again, but I was rapidly bleeding to death from lacerations to my knees and elbows sustained in the two bouts of greyhound wrestling. (Shorts and T-shirt and rough tarmac make a bad combination.)

Enter George the Wonder Dog. Somewhat bemused by all this unprecedented kerfuffle he ambled over and allowed me to remove his collar and slip it onto the now more or less quiescent hound. With dogs reassembled I limped back up the road and located the victim, who turned out to be a visiting in-law of one of my several hitherto unknown neighbours. I think they took pity on me, covered in blood (mine) and all that, so I got away with a £40 vet's bill for patching up the terrier, and no prosecution. Facing my daughter's wrath was another matter, but I think we'll draw the proverbial veil over that bit.

Another recent canine encounter proved to be almost as bloody. Driving through a neighbouring village early one dismal morning I spied a bedraggled, muddy terrier standing disconsolately by the side of the road. I stopped to appraise the situation. The collarless little dog had obviously spent the night out, perhaps after getting lost down a badger hole so, with no means of identifying him, I decided to phone the Law and leave it to them.

As I walked back to the car the little chap trotted along behind me, looking expectant. Touched, I resolved to take him home with me before calling the appropriate authority. I opened the door, told George to budge up a bit, and reached down to help the little critter into the car. By way of gratitude he sprang up and fastened his nasty little teeth onto my thumb like a spiteful ferret, and a good smack round the ear with my free hand was necessary to secure my release. I got back in the car and drove off. The little bugger might still be there for all I know.

A quite different local 'character' of the dog world was Barkley. (Shouldn't there be a law against awful-pun names? No dog deserves it.) Border collie x spaniel is always a dubious proposition, all too often inheriting the worst of both breeds rather than the best, and Barkley was no exception, being wildly unpredictable and occasionally nipping hapless visitors for no reason at all. But his real penchant was for surreptitiously stealing certain household items and burying them in the garden. Margarine tubs, full or otherwise, and tea-towels were his favourites. When I renovated his owners' garden we found no fewer than twenty-seven of the former and twenty-four of the latter. And one brassiere. This was of particular interest as the lady of the house was, shall we say, of ample proportions in the bra department, while the half-buried item was clearly of insufficient capacity. Its lightweight, lacy construction suggested, perhaps, a rather younger woman.

The three sons of the house were closely questioned but rejected outright the idea of a Prince Charming/Cinderella-type quest among the maidens of the village. The provenance of the buried bra remains a mystery to this day and Barkley, sadly no longer with us, certainly isn't telling.

And so to George, the ultimate Somerset dog. He had been 'rescued' from neglectful Travellers by a 'proactive' local rescue centre and, after extensive Gestapo cum dating-agency interrogation, I was allowed to adopt him. He became my companion, confidante and henchdog for over a decade.

He was certainly handsome, considered by his liberators to be a unique mix of collie, Alsatian and lurcher. He could out-run all but the quickest sight-hounds, out-think any collie and vanquish all comers in single combat. Aggressive Alsatians, corgis and even an English bull-terrier were taught some manners by way of his original retributive techniques, though it must be said that he never started fights - only finished them.

George was gentle and tolerant with all children and puppies, and even with most adults as long as they weren't wearing uniforms. He could run down rabbits, snatch pheasants from the air and charm the ladies with his good looks and gentlemanly demeanour. There will never be another George. I am rarely accused of being sentimental, but his ashes still sit on a shelf in my office.

Which is not to detract in any way from my current canine companion. Roxie is the thoroughly beautiful deerhound lurcher kindly given to me by 'a man in a pub', as described elsewhere. She is another canine couch potato, typical of her breed but, when on the loose, her pace and grace are a joy to behold. Her lawlessness occasionally causes some embarrassment (no cat is safe within half a mile) but, when not on the rampage, she is an absolute delight. She is my trusty companion on the walks described here.

Between George and Roxie, I enjoyed an all-too-short interlude with Mac, another rescue-centre special. Of unknown provenance, this gentle giant may have been some sort of Alsatian x Rottweiler, but his oddly stripy flanks suggested a bit of hyena. Despite his rather fearsome appearance he was the complete 'softy', and his gentleness endeared him to one and all. Sadly, after only a couple of years with me, he succumbed very suddenly to kidney tumours. He was a grand dog, and another example of how lucky I've been with my canine chums.

So that's just a few notable Somerset dogs, as delightful and variable as the countryside they occupy.

Brean Down. Bastion of the Bristol Channel.

Hinkley Point nuclear power station. Why Here?

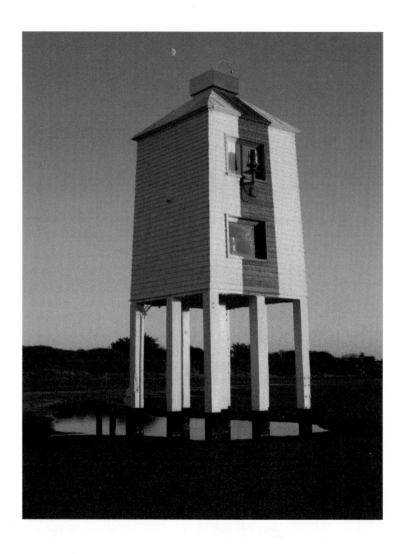

Lighthouse at Burnham on Sea. Still winking at passing mariners.

The blue anchor. Oddly at Watchet, not Blue Anchor.

Coastal geology in all its glory.

Blue Anchor promenade.

Ker Moor pilings. Once sea defences now like rotten teeth.

Roxie with acorn / coconut.

The Minehead Monstrosity. Your guess….

Exmoor and Brendon

County Gate to Withypool via Simonsbath

With Geoff

First get to County Gate! An early-ish bus from Bishops Lydeard to Minehead soon filled up with push-chairs, small children, large mothers and, of course, Roxie the Longdog. The gangway of this bus seemed unusually narrow, so she stood all the way, looking grumpy and occasionally grimacing at the raucous repartee of the young mothers. On reaching Minehead we disembarked with some relief, with time for a quick coffee in a pavement café before boarding a much nicer bus with a few other walkers heading for County Gate via the famously steep Porlock Hill.

Leaving the bus at County Gate we set off along the border over well-cropped pasture heading roughly south towards Malmsmead, dropping down the side of a steep combe to cross an ancient bridge over Badgworthy Water. Here we joined the Samaritans Way on the Devon side of the river and started up the beautiful wooded valley past the prettily-named Cloud Farm over on the Somerset side. The woodland gradually petered out as we entered a steep-sided, grassy gorge ominously labelled on the map as Doone Country. It seems unusual for fiction to feature in the Ordnance Survey but, for anyone unfamiliar with the work of R D Blackmore, the novel Lorna Doone, set on Exmoor in the 17th century, concerns a tribe of murderous villains, the eponymous Doones, eventually vanquished by our Somerset hero Gert Jan Ridd. It is reassuring to note that Doone Country appears to be on the Devon side.

Here a nameless stream joins the river from the west through a clearing once occupied by a medieval village, and at this point we left the Samaritans Way and climbed out of the combe around the west side of Badgworthy Hill onto the boggy grasslands of high Exmoor, with the first Cuckoo of the year calling heartily from the Hawthorns in the valley. Then it was a steep descent to Hoccombe Water which marks the border as it runs east to west. (This anomalous corner, projecting out of Somerset after a border change some time towards the end of the 18th century, required a trip to the Devon Records Office for an explanation. Alas, there was none.) A stone wall follows the stream on the Devon side, but anything worthy of the name of footpath or track was woefully lacking, and the going underfoot was seriously nasty. Even Roxie looked less than comfortable scrambling among the peat hags along the steep sides of the valley and stepping cautiously across several boggy tributary streams along the way. After what seemed like miles but is, in fact, no more than one, we made the relatively gentle climb up to Brendon Two Gates where the B3223 crosses the border over a rattling cattle-grid.

We collapsed for a lunch break on a boggy, grassy bank on the other side of the road where we seemed to be on top of the world, with the glory of high Exmoor stretching away in every direction. The only signs of human activity here are the single fence marking the border and the occasional vehicle clattering over the cattle-grid, though the number of standing stones, tumuli, cairns and the remains of settlements suggest that this high, remote moorland was well-populated in ages past. Perhaps, like a reciprocal of the 'summer people' of the Somerset Levels, the Neolithic and Bronze Age Somersetians hereabouts exploited the upland grazing in the summer months and retreated to the sheltered valleys through the harsh winters.

After Roxie had taken a final slurp from the peaty brown water in a pool between the hags we headed off across the boggy tussocks making uneasy walking westward along the border line. The terrain on the Devon side looked grassier so we slipped through a convenient gate before descending a steep combe marking the upper reaches of Farley Water. The climb out of here was a real gasper, even steeper than the memorable haul from Glenthorne to County Gate a couple of weeks ago. Here, we climbed fifty or sixty metres vertically in something under one hundred metres according to the map, and that is *steep!*

(This is probably a good time to mention the Walking Pole Saga. My companion, Geoff, is a veteran traveller of the first order and, inexplicably, a devoted user of a walking pole. Here we differ, as I find the wretched things to be an irritating encumbrance at best, and really nothing more than the 'serious' walkers' badge of authenticity. When we discovered that he had left it behind when we set out this morning his heart-rending feigned distress was matched by my relief. Now, at appropriate moments such as this precipitous climb, he delights in pointing out how much easier it would be with the assistance of the magic stick.)

Once breathing and heart-beat rate had returned to near normal we pressed on across the northern flank of Exe Plain before descending to the land-mark 'Hoar Oak Tree' at the bottom of yet another steepish combe. The original tree, which was part of a line of oaks marking the boundary of the Exmoor Forest, fell in 1658 and, while the others have mostly gone unmarked, this one has been replanted, most recently in 1917. The present incumbent, it must be said, is not a particularly impressive specimen. At this point we had decisions to make. The border continues westward for about two miles across unpleasantly un-footpathed terrain before turning sharply south at Saddle Gate where it is joined by the Tarka Trail. This would be the

purist's border-following route without doubt but would mean that
our arrival at our overnight stop at Simonsbath would certainly be
after dark and, possibly and disastrously, after closing time. The
latter consideration clinched it, though at Geoff's insistence and as a
token of good intent, we climbed about another half-mile along the
border to the remains of Hoar Oak Cottage. This marks the site of
temporary shepherds' huts dating from the 18th century and
probably long before, becoming permanent stone-built dwellings in
the 19th century. Now fenced off and in a dangerous state of
disrepair it must have been one of the most remote and inaccessible
habitations in this part of the moor. Sitting on the remains of a wall
for a quick tea-break we pondered on the lives of the people who
lived here in these rolling uplands close under the sky so long ago.

A little reluctantly we returned to the Tree and followed the Two
Moors Way southward on a course more or less parallel to the border
which is a mile or two away to the west. A Cuckoo glided ahead of
us and alighted on a Hawthorn tree no more than 20 yards away
before launching into his song while a pair of Meadow Pipits,
favourite targets of the Cuckoo's surrogate egg-laying, mounted a
brave attack. But the Cuckoo sang on regardless while his tiny
victims fluttered about his head.

We made our way steadily up the steep-sided combe on a
comfortable, grassy path for a mile, emerging at the top to find the
confluence of five paths at Exe Head. The open high moors rolled
away in all directions at about 450m above sea level and, literally,
this must be about as close as you get to heaven in Somerset unless
you're on top of Dunkery Beacon. Three of the five paths radiating
out from this point are National Trails (Two Moors Way, Tarka Trail
and Macmillan Way) but, as with some of our other encounters with
National Trails, the waymarking was poor or absent altogether. My
compass was called upon to make one of its rare appearances and,
under its guidance, we set off across the boggy top of Dure Down on
what we hoped is the Two Moors Way. Some of the irregularities in

the soggy surface are, apparently, the legacy of peat cutting which was practised here from medieval times, but that was little consolation when it came to stumbling through them. After negotiating a couple of poorly-marked gates we began the descent over 'improved' pasture towards the top of Lime Combe, the penultimate leg of the day's trek to Simonsbath. The last stretch of the combe runs through woodland which appeared to be a plantation of Sycamores, and we wondered why anyone would deliberately have installed these much-maligned immigrants on such a scale.

We hit the B3358 coming in from the west, crossed it, and joined a permissive path following the River Barle to Simonsbath Bridge. In the fading light this was a delightfully pretty spot after the sweeping openness of the high moor, and we paused on the ancient stone bridge before making our way up the hill to our goal - the Exmoor Forest Inn. Dumping our packs and boots by the door we headed for the bar without delay, where Roxie stretched out full-length on the floor and lapsed into exhausted semi-consciousness, barely raising her head to inspect the two resident spaniels bidding her welcome. The willingness of the staff to step over/around her (and the provision of a large dog-bed in my room) confirmed this as a thoroughly dog-friendly establishment. A pint or two of decent cider and a hearty dinner of venison pie completed a tough but hugely enjoyable day.

And having enjoyed the venison here in the heart of Somerset's hunting country, this is probably as good a time as any to reveal what some of my compatriots might see as a bit of hypocrisy if not downright treachery. I consider myself to be a very far cry from being anything resembling a 'veggie' or bunny-hugger, but I see the practice of chasing large mammals to death with a pack of dogs as demeaning, nasty and sad. The excuses put forward by the pro-hunters are pathetic and completely unconvincing to any knowledgeable countryman, and the quicker this unpleasant activity is totally banned the better. (Note that the Hunting Act introduced by the repellent, slimy, war-mongering Blair and his toadying crew had little or no effect.) Enjoy your venison by all means but despatch it humanely with a marksman's bullet. I did say there might be a rant or two.

It had to happen sooner or later. In the morning, looking out of the window I faced a low, grey sky and steady Exmoor rain. Nothing for it but a good breakfast and on with the waterproofs, including Roxie's unflattering but effective fluorescent yellow raincoat. Fortified with sausages she made no objection as we set off to the south-east along the beautiful Barle valley through what is moderate drizzle by Exmoor standards.

After about 20 minutes of easy going the path leaves the river to skirt around the north side of Flexbarrow, a prominent 'hump' that rears up out of the valley floor. With its top at about 340m this must be a geological feature rather than one of human origin, but more of that later. The path returns to the river where we found the fenced-off remains of the Wheal Eliza mine, with its long and sometimes unsavoury history. Unsuccessful attempts to extract minerals have been made here from as long ago as the 16th century, culminating in the industrial mania and blinkered greed of the 19th. Between 1845 and 1854 great efforts were made to find the erroneously-reported rich copper ore with no success, followed by further attempts to drag out viable iron between 1856-7 with similar results. One can only shrink in horror at the thought of what might have happened in this beautiful valley if those Victorian barbarians had succeeded. Perhaps today it would resemble Merthyr Tydfil, so it's thanks be to the gods of Exmoor.

But the most infamous piece of history concerning the mine is the story of the drunkard and ne'er-do-well William Burgess who, in 1858, murdered his 7-year old daughter and cast her body down the disused mine-shaft. When the body was eventually discovered, mainly due to the persistence of the local clergyman, the murderer's excuse was that he resented the two shillings and sixpence he was paying for her keep. He was hanged in Taunton in January 1859.

Putting Mr Burgess behind us we pressed on through the rain to the Iron Age hill-fort named on the map as Cow Castle. This is another conical hump similar to Flexbarrow, but this one is topped by a 2m rampart dating from about 1000 BC. These small fortifications pose a bit of a puzzle for historians, but the current popular theory is that they were temporary defences necessitated by an increasing population which obliged the locals to repel land-grabbing incomers. Could there be a lesson here for modern Somersetians?

Having breezed down this lovely valley our conscience called us back to the border a mile and a half away, so we crossed the Barle at a convenient ford and headed west, climbing an unnamed combe to regain the high moor. As we came upon the track leading to Horsen Farm we found a lamb stuck between the high banking formerly used as the field boundary and the modern stock-fence reinforcing it. While Geoff held on to the enthusiastic Roxie I managed to extract the lamb and returned it to the flock, inflicting only minor vandalism on the stock-fence and minor injuries on myself.

Leaving the track, we turned south on a supposed bridleway across high, boggy, peat-hag-ridden, nasty and severely-fenced fields. At one point the crude, blue-painted way-markers let us down and we found ourselves literally 'cornered' by the high banks, stock-fence and barbed wire which make up the accepted field boundaries in these parts. After Geoff had almost emasculated himself negotiating the barrier we recognised the impossibility of getting Roxie through, so a bit of step-retracing was required before we could find a suitable gateway. After one more squelchy field had been negotiated we were more than relieved to find ourselves on a track leading to Sherdon Farm. The latter turned out to be a large, semi-derelict farm house which was clearly a significant feature in its prime, but now the holes in the roof and the plastic ornaments in the window suggested a drastic decline in its fortunes. We descended the track to the picturesque Sherdon Bridge, passing the pretty Sherdon Cottage which sports a prominent "No Hunt Vehicles" notice on its gate. I salute the courage of the inhabitants whose stand must be less than popular in an area where chasing wild animals to death with a pack of dogs is considered normal behaviour.

The climb up the track from Sherdon Bridge seemed interminable, but eventually we reached a road which, we earnestly hoped, would take us to the border and, more importantly, to the Sportsman's Inn for lunch. After a mile of almost deserted road we were not disappointed. Once again, we deposited packs, boots and, this time, waterproofs in the porch and, once again, Roxie reclined at full-length on the floor of the bar. We were the only inmates so her elongate, recumbent form caused no inconvenience. The genial landlord and his son engaged us in cheerful conversation while supplying excellent local cider and well-filled baguettes - cheddar cheese and cider chutney, of course. An hour or so later, and in fine good humour, we ambled down the road about 100 yards to cross the border and turned eastward at Sandyway Cross along another empty road for about a mile to White Post. Here we turned off onto a signposted bridleway leading north-east towards today's destination. The rain had gone, the sun had come out and all was very well with the world. I should, perhaps, mention here that Geoff, though a proud Irishman, has a fondness for cider that might even equal my own, and I'm almost sure that the extra pint at the Sportsman's was at his insistence.

After a short descent across a boggy field with no trace of a path we joined a track leading down to Upper Willingford Bridge which crosses Litton Water along which the border runs. We were back in Somerset. A long, steady climb took us back up to the 390m contour across more of the by now familiar boggy, tussocky pasture before we started the slow descent towards Withypool which we could just make out tucked prettily into the valley in the distance. The path passes close to an old, quartered field-system intriguingly labelled as

Tudball's Splatts on the map. The explanation of this odd name may be simple enough: Tudball may be a corruption of Theobald (once a common surname) while 'splatt' may derive from the Old German 'splatten', meaning to split, providing a reminder of our Saxon heritage. It seems likely, therefore, that at some time Mr Theobald split his portion of land into four,

The track connects with the road about half a mile short of Withypool so, as the road was deserted and we were close to our rendezvous time, we took the easy option and strolled down the tarmac into the delightfully pretty village. The elegant six-arch bridge crosses the Barle here, and while Geoff went off in search of our chauffeuse I led Roxie down to the river for a well-earned drink. The afternoon sun highlighted the ripples on the gin-clear water, and I am bound to wonder if this pretty spot might be even closer to Heaven than the high moors we have just left.

Circuit from Dulverton

With Chris

Having recognised that walking the whole of the actual border-line
is impossible and that public transport in rural Somerset is not
always accommodating, we settled for doing the best we could and
drove down to Dulverton. The plan was to take in as much as
possible of the odd little bulge in the county boundary which extends
southward down to Exbridge, but first we indulged in a hefty
breakfast at the Tantivy café. (The hunting reference, typical of
Dulverton, goes against the grain, but they do a sterling breakfast.)
We crossed the bridge over the Barle and set off north following the
river: This is the scenic route to take us back to the border where it
suddenly turns south at Castle Bridge.

Even on a damp, pale grey morning the walk along the Barle was a
delight by any standard. The steeply-sloping oak woodland was
alive with birdsong, with Blackbirds, Song Thrushes, Blackcaps,
Chaffinches, Robins and Wrens all having their say. At Marsh
Bridge the woodland becomes mainly beech interspersed with
patches of plantation conifers, and I was treated to the unusual sight
of Chris crawling about on the ground trying to photograph the
forest-floor flora which, he said, is "interesting". Still close to the
river we passed the intriguingly-named New Invention, which is a

riverside house dating from the 19th century. At that time the burgeoning 'nouveau' wealth generated by the industrial revolution enabled businessmen, mostly from London, to build hunting 'boxes' on Exmoor to emulate the 'sporting' gentry. Perhaps New Invention reflects the source of some of this wealth while its modern equivalent, all too apparent these days in the form of tarted-up cottages and 'modernised' fine old houses, might well be called Bankers' Bonanza.

To get back to the border we were obliged to leave the Barle at the foot of Mounsey Castle, an Iron Age hill-fort atop a steep, heavily-wooded knoll rising up from the river valley. A short distance to the north we could see Brewers Castle, another similar if smaller fortification. The purpose of these, and the other hill-top enclosures further up the Barle, is not fully understood, but they surely bear witness to the level of instability and violence prevalent here a millennium or so before Christ. The border turns abruptly south not far ahead of us along the river, but the first mile or so of this south-bound stretch is inaccessible without blatant trespassing, so we cut back along a lane to Hinam Cross, resisting, in passing, the temptation of the prettily-situated Hinam Farm which offers ice-creams and other local goodies. We turned west for another mile along the Exmoor National Park boundary to reach the aptly-named Five Cross Ways, then followed the border south along Oldway Road, bounded by high beech hedges. Roxie, ever alert, spotted a roe deer through a gateway, and pranced and danced on the lead to the next break in the hedge where she watched with grim resignation as her prospective quarry made its getaway across the field. The landscape along here can only be described as 'pretty' on both the Devon and Somerset sides of the road, being a succession of vividly green fields dotted with photogenic sheep.

After another mile or two we reached Hawkwell Cross and, drawn by the pub symbol on the map, we crossed the border to the west towards the village of East Anstey in Devon. In a rare moment of clairvoyance Chris expressed scepticism about the existence of this pub and, alas, he was right. The Froude Arms, as was, is clearly defunct, with only a rusty bracket high on the frontage suggesting its former function so, disappointed but unbowed, we retraced our steps to Hawkwell Cross. Here we made the decision to abandon the border to avoid excessive road-work (too much tarmac being unkind to a country-bred Longdog's feet) and headed east along the Exe Valley Way. This is the nearest Right of Way to the border, which turns east, parallel to our track, about a mile to the south, which prompted one of my familiar rants about restrictive land ownership, the iniquities of William the Conqueror, denial of access and so on. It seems somehow wrong that a Somersetian should be unable to walk the bounds of his own county and, I suppose, with due deference to equal opportunities and all that, this should apply to the natives of other counties on their home ground too. Chris is well used to this sort of stuff and gave every impression of listening with polite attention.

At West Knowle the Exe Valley Way leaves the road and joins the dismantled railway which once ran from Norton Fitzwarren near Taunton to Bampton and all points west. Opened in 1871 this line was part of the extensive rail network in this part of the world until, as with so many others, it fell foul of the whims of the demoniacal Dr Beeching in the 1960's. We climbed up onto a high embankment and marvelled at the work which must have gone into the construction of this line without the aid of heavy machinery nearly 150 years ago. To the south some small, marshy fields rise up to woodland, and here we spotted a roe deer in her orange summer coat gazing at us through a mouthful of buttercups. Fortunately, she kept quite still, and Roxie failed to notice her.

The track was lined with overgrown sallows and scrub forming a green tunnel, so we pressed on until a break in the vegetation afforded a view over the boggy fields, and we stopped for a late lunch sitting on a fallen tree. With rain threatening we soon moved on, and after another mile we left the rather dismal remains of this sad old railway line and cut through onto the road. This led us shortly into Brushford where we stopped at the church to don our rain-gear, including Roxie's unflattering high-vis coat. Proceeding through deserted Brushford in the drizzle Chris remarked rather enigmatically that "It must be impossible to have fun here", and I have to agree that this uncharacteristically harsh comment seems entirely justified, despite the lamp-post notice telling us that the village hall becomes a pub every other Friday. Doubtless there is some charm to be found somewhere here, but this road, flanked by newish, well-kept, characterless houses isn't it. We were mightily relieved to reach the end of it, crossing the main road and pausing on the impressive bridge over the Barle.

If we were to continue on this road for another half-mile we would meet the border as it runs back up along the River Exe, but that would have to wait for another day. Instead, we turned off north on a footpath across the fields alongside the Barle on our way back to Dulverton. I unleashed Roxie, letting her bound away over the long grass on a leg-stretching run before returning to trot along the riverside path, clearly enjoying the abundance of dog scents. Despite the level ground here the river is fast-moving and broken, and it was easy to imagine the famous Barle salmon forging their way upstream through the rapids, and as the path turns away from the river an elegantly curved weir spans the flow. On the map this is labelled as 'Salmon Trap' which, apparently, was built in the 1960's to aid in the conservation of the noble fish, though I have been unable to find out just how. Sitting on a rock in the middle of the roaring torrent a female Goosander provided our rarity of the day.

Just after the salmon-challenging weir, the path eases its way into Dulverton along a tarmac track, emerging conveniently almost opposite the Bridge Inn. The rain had stopped so we sat outside this comfortable, dog-friendly house to enjoy a pint of half-decent cider while Roxie stretched out as usual, receiving her customary admiration from passers-by. Even when recumbent and semi-conscious she seems to attract attention, which she acknowledges with no more than a languidly raised head.

Apart from the delightful setting of Dulverton and the first stretch along the Barle this has not been the most spectacular of our border ventures so far, but the 'Dulverton Bulge' is part of Somerset and so demanded a visit. It is sobering, perhaps humbling, to reflect that this undeniably lovely area seems rather 'ordinary' in comparison with some of the breath-taking country we have crossed in previous walks, but then, that's Somerset.

Dulverton to Wiveliscombe

With Chris & Lottie

This stretch will take us from the point where we left the border near Brushford to follow the line as closely as possible as it runs west to east before plunging south towards the Blackdowns. This is the narrowest part of the county, only about 15 miles from here to the coast in the north and runs through what promises to be some of the most beautiful country we have seen so far. It's going to be a long day.

We drove to Wiveliscombe on a pale grey Exmoor morning in time for the 8.47 bus to Dulverton. We were the only passengers, so Roxie could stretch out undisturbed in the aisle while we enjoyed a picturesque helter-skelter, roller-coaster of a ride through the hills and valleys of the Exmoor fringe, arriving in Dulverton just before 9.30. After a fortifying coffee and cake, we retraced our steps back down the Barle to Brushford bridge where we left off last time, then headed off east to meet the A369 at the enigmatically-named Snapbox. (Yorkshire friends tell me that in their language a snap-box is a container for a packed lunch, but how this point on the Somerset/Devon border came to be so named remains a mystery.) Chris was keen to get a photograph of the two adjacent county posts, so I hauled back the foliage half-concealing the Devon sign and inadvertently ended up in the picture. The wind-blown hair makes me look like a demented Art Garfunkel, so this one will *not* be retained.

The border heads off east with no access for us, so we opted for a lane which runs parallel to it only a couple of hundred yards to the north. With the steep, wooded hillside named as Pixy Copse to our right and the River Haddeo meandering through the valley to our left this is a gaspingly beautiful stretch. In the middle of the almost unnaturally pretty hamlet of Bury we left the road and began to climb steeply up Haddon Lane, a deep, muddy, sunken track with the remains of a stream running down the middle. A couple walking down the lane earnestly warned us of impending dangers: steep inclines, bottomless mud and lightning, but their London accents suggested a degree of hypersensitivity to rural dangers so, after thanking them for their concern, we pressed on regardless. Instead of insurmountable hazards Chris found a large chunk of half-rotten wood which, he claimed, resembled an Ichthyosaur skull. His attempt at photography resulted in a spectacular slide down the slippery bank, leaving the 'Ichthyosaur' and the dogs looking on with apparent indifference and me with a *schadenfreude* grin.

We reached the top otherwise unscathed and walked along the contour through open, mixed woodland with glorious views through the trees towards the border about half a mile away to the south. Under the convenient cover of a huge beech we stopped for lunch as the rain started with serious intent, and Roxie stretched out in the dry leaf-litter between the massive roots grasping the stony soil. A little way up the hill behind us is the spectacular view-point on Haddon Hill, home to the rare Heath Fritillary butterfly, but we resisted the temptation of a detour as we were well aware that we still had a long way to go to Wiveliscombe. Instead, as the rain kindly stopped and the sun came out, we took the road south over Frogwell Cross then turned east on a bridleway parallel to the border.

A sloping field led us to an unexpected drive-way running down to the startling edifice which is Leigh Barton. This is a collection of huge stone barns and a substantial house, with the footpath running through the middle, the lot showing contradictory signs of opulence and decrepitude. Dating from medieval times, this was once a grange of Cleeve Abbey, enlarged in 1627 then rebuilt in 1811, but its present status is unclear although there are signs of current habitation. Luckily, Chris was ahead at this point so he scattered the herd of cats lounging about in the yard before Roxie caught sight of them. (Her dislike of these odious, bird-killing, garden-fouling little brutes is even greater than mine, and the sight of even one of them will send her into murderous hysterics. Lottie, on the other hand, is unaccountably unmoved by these nasty little creatures, despite her tendency to attack pretty much anything else.)

Leaving the yard, we descended a little-used bridleway down a deep gulley leading to a delightful, boggy valley surrounded by steep-sided hills. We crossed the stream and climbed the grassy slope, looking back across the valley where four red deer grazed peacefully, one of them sporting the emerging spikes witnessing his first full year of staghood. We followed the contour (225m) then descended into the very pretty but regrettably publess village of Skilgate tucked between more steep-sided hills. The roads hereabouts are usually deserted, so strolling along the tarmac for a while through this beautiful valley was no hardship. We stopped for a second lunch by the roadside before turning south at Blackwell to follow the border along the River Batherm to the tranquility of Batherm Bridge, where the only sounds were the rippling of the river and the drifts of birdsong from the woods across the water.

The border turns sharply east at the bridge so we followed it along the road past the village of Raddington for a good mile before turning off on a footpath which climbs up through dense woodland known as Batscombe Copse, where the border turns abruptly south.

Here the rain returned with real malice so we donned all available waterproofs and abandoned the border for the day, heading north on a bridleway at the start of the long haul back to Wiveliscombe. As we passed over Chubworthy Cross and began the ascent up Stonebridge Lane to the hill-top village of Chipstable the clouds passed on and the sun obligingly came out. We paused only to shed the waterproofs outside the pretty 15th century church before climbing out of the village and turning east along the hill-top road towards Wivey. (In retrospect I am at a loss to know why we ignored the bridleway from Chipstable to Marshes Farm, but ignore it we did, with a cost of about a mile.) The most notable features along the road were a trio of turkeys and a brace of guinea fowl wandering free under the towering beeches. At this stage Roxie was too tired to notice, so the gobblers were left in peace.

The road winds steeply down another lovely valley to Bulland Ford, where we declined the somewhat hazardous crossing of the River Tone and stayed on the west side of the river, following it down through pretty woodland to the road at Marshes Farm. A lane running parallel to the 'New Road' (the B3227) took us to Fleed Cross where we scampered across the highway at the top of the hill and took to the footpath which would lead us back to Wiveliscombe. From here on the 260m contour we had a glorious view across Taunton Vale to the Quantocks in the distance, with Wivey sparkling in the evening light down below us. We ambled down over the sloping fields, pausing only to exchange greetings with a couple of friendly horses, passed through a farmyard and across one final stream, then up a gentle incline past the recreation ground and onto the road.

We hit The Square at seven o'clock, and I have rarely been so happy to see The Bear ahead. As predicted, this was a long day, but we had enjoyed the privilege of walking through some of the most beautiful countryside in the county, and hence in the country if not in the world. Roxie adopted her customary horizontal position on the bar floor while we raised our glasses of Wivey-brewed Exmoor Ale to toast another glorious day around the border.

Waterrow to Wellington

With Howard

The intention for this stage was to pick up the border where we left off last time at Batscombe Copse and hence to Tracebridge, but this would have entailed a lengthy road-walk which would be unkind to a dog's feet. We decided to cheat just a little and to follow the West Deane Way south from Waterrow, running about a mile east of the border itself.

Our kindly chauffeuse dropped us off on a tidy stone bridge over the rocky River Tone in a deep, wooded valley near Boucher's Farm. The boggy, upsy-downsy path, with wooden causeways and frequent flights of steps, rises steeply up from the river through towering ash wood with Hazel understory and a profusion of Hart's Tongue ferns giving an almost tropical feel. Ahead, the huge stone pillars of Waterrow viaduct, a part of Brunel's old railway, rise above the tree-tops to a height of 32m. The stone-work looks as good as new, and we marvelled at this breath-taking feat of Victorian engineering, the three pillars once carrying the track 148m to span the valley. It is almost impossible to imagine multiple tons of steam train passing way up there over our heads, and we agreed that the little chap with the tall hat must certainly have been a genius and his workers must have been heroes.

The woodland changed abruptly from ash to beech as we moved along the contour, before we emerged into open fields through a kissing-gate topped, surprisingly, with an empty coffee mug. A charming lady with a sturdy spaniel reclaimed it as she appeared from the wood behind us, which solved the mystery of the mug and afforded Roxie the opportunity for a little canine socialising. We followed the spaniel across the open hillside and descended to a small collection of cottages and 'conversions', then followed a lane to what we took to be Hagley Bridge. Here the map and what we could see before us seemed to be rather at odds so, in the absence of any meaningful signposts, we pressed on regardless, following the Tone along another dramatically steep-sided valley with the river a good 30m below us. The path became impassably boggy so we scrambled up a bank and took to the fields where we were joined by a procession of curious heifers. They seemed to be taking a keen interest in Roxie, but she afforded them only a disdainful glance and plodded on stoically.

The map suggested that we had arrived at Tuck's Farm where the path kinks sharply down to the river. Leaving the cattle behind we slid down the slippery slope to a marshy meadow and followed the river bank for a short distance as the map dictated, only to encounter a chained and padlocked gate. I climbed over and scrambled through the undergrowth to locate the predicted track while Howard, ever confident and optimistic, effortlessly lifted the passively compliant Longdog over the gate and followed me through. I could not but admire the ease with which he levitated 35kg of hairy hound, but he assured me that his own wriggling collies, thankfully left at home today, present much more of a challenge in such circumstances.

Still slightly at odds with the map we climbed a slippery, rocky track reminiscent of some of our expeditions in Zambia long ago, then traversed another steep, wooded hillside before arriving abruptly and indisputably on the road at the delightfully pretty Stawley

Bridge. The crystal-clear, sparkling water dancing over the rocks just cried out for running salmon but, alas, not today. Unfortunately the West Deane Way leaves the river here, so we headed for the border a mile and a bit to the south on the circuitous road to Ashbrittle. We took a well-earned cider-break in a gateway at the top of the hill, with glorious views back over the village of Stawley and ahead to the Blackdowns in the distance, and conceded that our proposed target for today, Wellington Monument, looked an awful long way off.

The tiny village of Ashbrittle is a real delight, with most of the lovely old cottages lacking that regrettable 'done up' look beloved of in-comers in so many Somerset villages these days. The vehicles parked outside included some aged vans and battered pick-ups instead of the all-too-common shiny silver 4x4's, suggesting that some real, working people might live here. The old red phone-box is full of books and clearly serves as the library, and someone had conveniently left a football on the little village green, allowing us a brief kickabout before we headed off in the direction of Tracebridge. The impression of traditional rural life was somewhat dispelled as we passed Ashbrittle Stud, now the home of a well-known stable of race-horses. Obviously, the product of in-coming money on a grand scale, this is the only 'farm' I have ever seen where the wooden field gates are freshly painted a fetching dove grey, each bearing its own prettily-lettered label: Upper Cow Field, Second North Land etc., and all enclosed in top-class close-board fencing which would do credit to any grand garden. Whew!

A confluence of roads in the valley bottom at Tracebridge marked our return to the border, which we followed up the hill past an old quarry now serving as a timber-yard. A handsome lady in a passing Land Rover stopped to admire the Longdog - she has one at home - and lamented my admission, under interrogation, that I have deprived this magnificent creature of the opportunity to reproduce. In my defence I quoted the advice of my beloved vet: "Unless you want a permanent house-full of assorted puppies I should have her done if I were you. If she fancies a bit of fun in the woods there's not much you can do to stop her, is there?" The Land Rover lady was barely placated but took the point. One has some interesting conversations with strangers on remote country roads hereabouts.

At this point we took a deliberate detour on a footpath north-east to the village of Appley where, I happen to know, The Globe will always provide suitable lunch-time refreshment. A sturdy baguette (bacon and black pudding, in deference to my Yorkshire companion) and a pint of Exmoor saw us fit, and we were ready for the road again. As we left the very pleasant garden Roxie received more admiration from a couple of ladies at a nearby table and acknowledged their cooing with a graceful stretch.

(Aside: It really is a shame that so many otherwise excellent Somerset pubs are unable to offer decent local cider. The explanation/excuse is that the lack of demand is such that the 15- or 20-litre barrels 'go off' before the contents are sold, meaning that the customers aren't drinking enough. Impasse. Perhaps the worthy landlords/ladies might try cutting the price a bit, thus encouraging the clientele to try the real thing instead of the nasty, fizzy stuff usually on offer.)

The border meanders south-east from here and we followed it along the road to Greenham where we crossed the Tone on the 19th century iron bridge, appropriately painted green. The river makes a sharp U-turn just south of Greenham so is now running north or, as Howard put it, "the wrong way" as it passes under the bridge. On the right we passed the unusual if not quite beautiful church of St Peter, in the Gothic style favoured in the late 19th century. This one was consecrated in 1860, and what it lacks in antiquity and architectural appeal it makes up for in the beauty of its valley setting. The road passes over the barely-visible remains of the old Grand Western canal before we turned off to the south to get back to the border. As we passed Gamlin's Farm we were struck by the unusual combination of a caravan park and a large-scale chicken farm, the presence of the latter being marked by its unmistakeable stench. While I am sympathetic towards and even enjoy most countryside smells, this one was a bit much for me, and the idea of a holiday in this atmosphere is not altogether appealing.

At the next crossroads we encountered the worst hazard of the whole trip so far: There must be a new, active quarry in the vicinity, as we were confronted by a convoy of huge gravel trucks thundering past at a rate of one about every thirty seconds. There was no escape, so we trudged on up the road, flattening ourselves against the bank whenever a juggernaut threatened. I must add that the drivers of these beasts were both alert and considerate, so the potential danger was minimised, and Roxie was completely unmoved by the roaring monsters as she plodded along with lofty disregard.

After only half a mile of this, though it seemed like rather more, we turned off thankfully on what we hoped was a neat detour to avoid the dangers of the impending A38. This took us on a footpath around an old quarry harbouring a boggy lake, round the bustling Shippen Farm and up some steep fields to meet the main road at White Ball. We dodged the traffic with ease and picked up a little-used footpath on which, I remember, I installed a couple of squeezer-stiles back in my contracting days. The path took us across corn fields and through an archway under the main railway line before joining the road to Sampford Arundel. In this lovely, rolling country we had sweeping views in all directions, including a sight of the Monument which we were bound to recognise was still a very long way off. We decided to terminate the border-following mission for the day and turn north-east to Wellington. Modern technology, to be shunned whenever possible, has its uses at times, and allowed us to communicate with our chauffeuse to arrange a pick-up point.

As we approached Wellington via Pleamore Cross, the softer contours were strikingly different from the steep hills and deep, wooded valleys we had passed through just a few hours ago. From the 100m contour we looked across the vale of Taunton Deane with its gentle arable curves and appreciated again the contrasts which make up this wonderful county.

Interlude 3

Alien Encounter

I'd only stopped to pick up a dead pheasant on the way home from work one Friday evening. (There's nothing wrong with fresh road-kill.) The shiny black Audi came around the corner just a bit too fast and slammed on the brakes, stopping a good six inches short of my tail-gate. The bloke got out, eyes a-popping and looking a bit pale.

"Can you move back a bit," I said. "I want to put this one in the back."

He looked at me, and at the dead pheasant, and seemed to have a problem opening his mouth.

"You could have killed us," he said or, rather, gasped.

"No," I said, nice and gently, "_You_ could have killed us. This is a lane, mate, not the bloody motorway."

"Now look here ..." he started.

"I am," I said, "and I can see somebody who was driving too bloody fast. Now move back a bit, there's a good chap. I want to get on home."

I don't know if he heard me, as there was a tractor coming down the hill in front of us. Right then, a bloody great silver 4x4 came around the corner and slammed on the anchors. You should have seen the Audi bloke jump. He was still in the air when the 4x4 gave his tail-end a bump, just enough to shunt him forward and give my old bus a bit of a tap.

The tractor had come up by then and stopped alongside. Old Gerald, grinning all over his ugly old face, surveyed the scene.

"You want to get a move on," he bellowed, " 'fore some bugger comes along and makes it a hat-trick."

The second bloke got out of the 4x4, looking around in a dazed sort of way.

"I say," he said. (Yes, he really said 'I say'.) "Shouldn't we move somewhere safer? I mean, if someone else comes round that corner ….."

Old Gerald looked down at me, still grinning. "You all right, my cocker? If you want a witness you know where I'm to. I'm off then." And he put the tractor half way up the bank and squeezed past the lot of us.

The two strangers seemed to have forgotten I was there. They were poking around at the back-end of the Audi and seemed to be getting along just fine. It's funny, isn't it? You drop a couple of Martians on an alien planet - they've never met before, mind you - and they're mates right off. Never mind that one's just rammed the other's spaceship. I bet that if they'd had a shunt like that in London they'd be scrapping by now.

London? How did I know they came from London and not Mars? Come on. Just look at them.

Anyway, I'm thinking I might as well be off when I heard something coming up from behind. I could see what was going to happen so, quick as you like, I jumped in the car, slung the pheasant on the passenger seat, and took off. I didn't even look in the mirror, but I heard the bang. I had to stop, didn't I?

Stan had come trundling around the corner in his ancient Landie and tried to swerve round the silver thing. He nearly made it too, but his front bumper, long ago replaced by an old scaffolding pole, just caught the tail-end corner <u>and</u> the door the bloke had left open. Dear oh dear.

Now Stan is not known for his tact and diplomacy, far from it, and he gave them a right mouthful. The Landie was all right, of course, with not a scratch that you'd notice, but Stan was well aggrieved. I was fifty yards up the road but I could hear him from there. I could see him lean across and slide open the passenger-side window.

"That's a right effin' place to stop for a effin' chat," he roared. "You could get somebody effin' killed.

He crunched the old Landie into gear and drove off, stopping right alongside me.

"What do 'ee think of they buggers," he growled. "Thinks they owns the place. I dunno."

I looked back down the road. The 4x4's door was hanging off like a busted wing. One of the blokes was pointing and shouting as Stan chugged off up the hill and the other was on a mobile phone. I glanced back at the retreating Landie. The number plate was plastered in muck, so that was all right. I thought about it for a minute and seemed to remember something about 'leaving the scene of an accident' or some such, so I got in the car and backed up, stopping a good twenty yards clear of the Audi.

"I called the police," the Audi bloke was saying. I don't know if he was talking to me or not. "They weren't interested. If no-one was hurt, they said, it wasn't their problem. What the bloody hell are the police for round here?" I let that go.

"I should move if I were you," I said, "before another one comes along."

The 4x4 bloke pointed at the door and waved his arms about a bit. It was then that I noticed a woman and a few kids in the silver job, and a daffy-looking bird in the Audi. I was feeling a bit sorry for them by now. Must be native chivalry.

"Just move up the road a bit," I said, "and get away from this corner. Then we'll have a look at that door."

They both got in and shifted up behind me, and I got a bit of bailer twine out of the back. It didn't take a minute. I hoiked the door more or less back in place, tied one end of the twine to the handle and passed the other end to the bloke inside. With the twine passed round the back of the front seats and out through the passenger window I secured it to the passenger door handle. Easy.

"It might be a bit draughty," I told him, "but I daresay it'll get you where you're going."

The bloke stuck his head out of the window. "Thanks very much," he said. "Very decent of you."

"No trouble, mate," I said. And I pushed off home.

A couple of weeks later, on a Saturday evening, I was in the pub when I noticed the 4x4 chappie and his tribe sitting at a nearby table having a meal. (I can't abide kids in pubs, but that's another story altogether.) They genuinely didn't recognise me. I wonder, if I had a pair of green antennae sticking out of my head, whether they might have.

The Blackdowns

Sampford Moor to Forches Corner

Just me and the Longdog

Having abandoned the border around Peacehay last time out with Howard, I checked the map and found an all too familiar lack of Rights of Way on what should be the next stretch, with the M5 as an added disincentive. The best option seemed to be to pick up the border again in the vicinity of Sampford Moor, at 268m one of the higher spots on the Blackdowns. Just south of the Moor, according to the map, the road appears to pass under the motorway but, alas, it doesn't. Thwarted, I retraced my steps or, rather, my tyre tracks, and drove round via Wrangway to Crossways Farm from which I intended to walk a circuit back, just south of the border, to Sampford Point before returning to Crossways via Sampford Common. Ah, but the best laid plans ….

In warm sunshine we left the car and set out into Whitehall plantation, where I made my first mistake. The footpath which follows the border is clearly marked on the map but, somehow, I managed to ignore it and took a forestry track heading south. After nearly a mile of tall conifers interspersed with clearings where I counted adders a couple of months ago, I realised the error and turned back. (Serves me right for venturing so far into Devon.) The huge telecommunications aerial, visible on the map and from the ground, should have been a clue from the start, but I now used it as a guide and we got back on the right track. We left the plantation and started off across high, open moorland towards Sampford Point. The unintended detour had set us back an hour, so I cut the corner and headed back directly into Somerset across the Common.

The view to the north rolls away across the Vale of Taunton Deane, past Wellington and on to the Brendon Hills in the hazy distance: another 'on top of the world' moment. I unleashed the enthusiastic Roxie and she loped away, sniffing every heather tussock with obvious enjoyment. Another all-too-casual glance at the map suggested that our return path ran along the bottom of the steep incline ahead, so we took off down a rocky track towards the woods below. Unfortunately, we were a little further west than I thought and, in the grip of what I can only imagine to be hallucination, we decided on a tarmac lane leading north. (As this was only intended to be a short stroll I forbore to bring the compass. Idiot!) The rumble of the M5 ahead confirmed that we were pointing in the wrong direction (by approximately 180°) so, just a little confused, I sought directions in a convenient cottage. The lady of the house was pleasant enough and would, I'm sure, have been helpful but for her lack of spectacles. Her bleary-eyed partner, on the other hand, was a grumpy, truculent sod, but I was just about able to translate his grunts sufficiently to establish that some step-retracing was called for. As we left their garden Roxie spied a sneaking cat, and almost took me off my feet with an unexpected felicidal lunge but, perhaps for the best, the wretched thing slithered just out of range.

We plodded back up the hill onto Sampford Common and discovered a large pond in what was once an ancient enclosure. While Roxie took a well-earned drink, I marvelled again at the view across to Exmoor as a silent buzzard drifted past only a few feet over my head. Taking no more map-based chances we headed straight for the mast and were soon walking down the track which leads back to Crossways. A notice nailed to a tree warns cyclists to beware of a new gate ahead, and when we reached the bottom I could see why: It is the only anti-speeding-cyclist device I have ever seen, and a fine piece of kit it is. Spanning the track is a barrier about 20cm high, easy enough for a person, a horse or a Longdog to step over but disastrous for any speeding mountain-biker foolish enough to ignore the notice. I would dearly like to see these installed on some of my favourite Quantock tracks.

From a mile west of the Wellington Monument the border runs eastwards along a nominally unclassified road across the Blackdowns for another three or four miles to Forches Corner. Unclassified or not, this stretch is a combination of no verges, long straights, wicked bends and numerous junctions, so is a potential death-trap for walkers, which explains my decision to drive it. Cheating? Maybe, but better than ending up as yet more road-kill.

Back in the car along the border road I noticed the sign to the Wellington Monument to the left. This is a justified diversion, I think, so we parked up and started off on the well-worn, tree-lined avenue towards the Monument itself. As we left the car-park a little girl trotted up and regarded the Longdog with an appraising gaze. "Can I stroke her?" she asked and, as if in answer, Roxie rested her chin on the little girl's shoulder and received her tribute with customary dignity. The girl's mother arrived with a frail, elderly lady in a wheelchair, and the elegant hound basked in the attention of three generations.

It must be all of ten years since I last visited the Monument, and things have changed. If my memory serves me aright you could phone the custodian in advance and the tower would be unlocked to allow you to climb the countless narrow stairs to the top and view what seemed like the whole world from the three round 'windows'. This exercise was not for the claustrophobic, vertigoid or faint-hearted. Now, the Monument is surrounded by a high chain-link fence with the gates and door severely padlocked, the whole edifice being deemed unsafe in 2007. (Local lore has it that a cow once managed to get itself half-way up the tower, but I have yet to meet an eye-witness to learn how the adventurous bovine got down again.)

The construction was commenced in 1817 as "A Fitting Tribute to a Nation's Victorious Hero", namely the Duke of Wellington's sterling performance at Waterloo in 1815. Building started and stopped as the money came and went, but was finally completed in 1854, sadly two years after the bold Duke died. The enormous stone column, either 29, 43 or 53 metres tall depending on how you measure it, is in the form of a slender triangular-section spike reputedly in the shape of one of Wellington's bayonets. Not pretty, but certainly impressive as, apparently, the fifth highest monument of its kind in the world. The single huge cannon mounted on the north-west side is one of twenty-four originally intended to grace the site, but a series of fiascos led to the others getting lost along the way, and the single survivor was eventually installed in 1984.

Even from here on the ground at the base of the column, the view to the north should be magnificent but, in the years since I was last here, the trees surrounding the clearing have been allowed to grow so the vista is obscured, permitting only a glimpse of the distant Quantocks. Pity.

Returning to the car we drove the remaining three or four miles along the road to Forches Corner, where the border turns sharply south and the Merry Harriers sits in splendid isolation. It was six o'clock, and I found to my deep distress that the place didn't open until half-past. Bugger! After several hours of refreshment-free, somewhat disorderly walking I was in no state to wait for half an hour for a drink, so we headed for home and a pint of decent cider. On the way down from the heights of the Blackdowns I reflected that solitary walking, even with a Longdog, is far less entertaining than with well-chosen human company which, rather than distracting from observation of and absorption in the surroundings, enhances the connection.   It also encourages closer attention to the map-reading!

Forches Corner to Bishopswood

Me & Roxie again

This looked likely to be a tricky stretch of border running south from the Merry Harriers, with most of the footpaths on the Devon side, so I decided to make it a walk some/drive some venture, and Roxie agreed.

We started at the head of the Wiltown Valley, just in Devon, and parked in a convenient lay-by next to the entrance to a footpath which plunged into a conifer plantation. After only a couple of hundred yards on a little-used path we found ourselves unexpectedly on the edge of a populous but strangely quiet camp site, where the reserved demeanour of the few visible occupants suggested they may be an exclusive religious sect or some such. Pressing on, we negotiated a stile and attempted to follow the map as the path turned south, but it promptly petered out in a dense, boggy wood with no sign of a trail. This was not a good start, and I was reminded that I have never felt truly at home on the Blackdowns, nor in Devon for that matter.

We retraced our steps back to the car, attracting no attention or response from the morose campers, and drove down Downlands Lane, parallel to the valley and thankfully safely in Somerset again.

I was determined to have a real look at this Wiltown Valley with the border running along the bottom, so we pulled in at a footpath sign pointing more or less in the right direction to try our luck again. A sign-board informed us that this is the Rington Nature Reserve and a part of the Valley Heads Way, neither of which appeared on my rather elderly map, but we began the descent regardless, starting with a pleasant open woodland with extensive clearings. These appeared to have been grazed fairly recently, as witnessed by the cropped grass and wizened cow-pats, but there was no sign of livestock now.

As we approached the border in the valley bottom I paused to watch a beautiful Silver-Washed Fritillary cruising over the brambles before it settled to feed. This orange and black gem is one of the largest of the British butterflies and, to me, one of the loveliest. It was so quiet in this secluded valley that I could almost hear its wings.

We scrambled down a muddy bit of track and crossed a wooden bridge over a swampy stream into Devon. On this side the woodland was dense, mostly ash and chestnut, and in a small clearing near the stream there stood what appeared to be a rather dilapidated garden shed. The stack of firewood by the door and the cooking fire nearby implied recent occupation, but the stout padlock on the flimsy door told me that no-one was at home. A pity, as it would have been interesting to meet this isolated forest-dweller.

Climbing up a serviceable path through the wood we emerged at the top into a small field which led to the road labelled on the map as Applehayes Lane where we headed north for half a mile or so, looking for the footpath which would descend again into the valley and back into Somerset. On the corner where the footpath is supposed to leave the road, a couple of local worthies and a mini-digger were doing a bit of work on a cottage which was certainly in need of it. The pair stopped work as we approached, eyeing us up with what I imagined to be curiosity. (Not many 'strangers' round here I guess.) The elder of the two had the look of an ancient mariner, with a jaunty cap, a magnificent white beard and piercing, pale-blue eyes. He appraised the Longdog. "Doin' a bit of poachin' then?"

"No, not today," I told him. "I've just come across the border and I'm looking for the way back. I thought there was a footpath about here."

The other bloke, big and cheerful-looking, jerked a huge thumb over his shoulder.

"That's 'ee," he said, "but you won't be gettin' down there. He 'abn't been cleared in years." He pointed to what looked like a driveway next to the cottage. "You go on down there," he said. "That'll get you back over." I thanked them kindly and set off down the recommended track, skirting the half-acre or so of bare earth dotted with assorted ramshackle chicken-houses and a collection of equally assorted free-ranging poultry. Whatever goes on here is surely not the sort of 'lifestyle' which appears in the Sunday supplements, but has far more appeal.

The track/drive led to a couple of severely 'done up' houses with a selection of glossy cars outside. The footpath sign pointed straight ahead, seemingly through one of the gardens, but the map suggested that the way back into the valley and the border is down a high-banked tunnel of shrubbery following the bed of a stream. As we negotiated the slippery rocks, the dogs in the adjacent house became aware of our presence and started up an impressive chorus of deep, sonorous barks. Blood-hounds, Danes or Baskervilles by the sound of it and, either way, I was glad they were confined. Roxie is usually keen on canine company but showed no interest.

We reached the border at the bottom and splashed across the stream to find no trace of a path on the other side, though one features clearly on the map. (Here we go again.) The climb ahead through boggy woodland is severely steep, but we found a way around fallen branches and mossy tussocks to break out at the top into an area of chest-high tussock grass stretching away up a relatively gentle slope towards the road, we hoped. I have seen nothing quite like this since

Zambia, where the swampy 'dambos' provide a haven for wildlife of all sorts. Keeping a watchful eye open for buffalo and rhino we picked our way carefully through the tussocks in a generally upward direction and, after an interminable plod, eventually reached a field boundary which we followed back to Downlands Lane and the car.

The road to Smeatharpe, they say, is paved with good intentions, and mine was to drive to Middleton Mill or thereabouts then walk the bridleway to Smeatharpe and back in a circuit. This is quite feasible, according to the map, but having negotiated the twisty, sometimes precipitous jungley lanes past Brimley Cross into Devon, out again and along the border for a mile or two we found ourselves in a deep, narrow valley as near to the middle of nowhere as makes no difference. I found what is presumably the start of the bridleway, but it is unsigned and so overgrown that even Roxie shook her head and turned back to the car. This is a remote and beautiful bit of country but the paucity of access and lack of waymarking was doing nothing to reduce my Blackdownophobia. Thwarted again, we drove back out of the valley and circled around to the border at Smeatharpe, where it turns sharply north-east towards Churchinford. We were now once again on the high, flat plateau which makes some of the Blackdowns so dismal. I could see little point in tramping the footpath along the border across this tedious landscape so we opted to drive to Churchinford with a view to a lunch-stop.

Ostensibly pretty, the deserted village had the feel of a place waiting for the bandits to ride in. I stopped, hoping to see Clint Eastwood emerge from the pub with a cheroot between his teeth and a gun in his hand, but we were disappointed. Instead, the packs of snarling dogs confined in the backs of Land Rovers and pick-ups in the car park indicated that this is not a dog-friendly establishment, so we retreated to a lay-by up the road and shared a sandwich. Most of the buildings here are either new or nastily 'done up', some sporting thoroughly inappropriate names like 'Highland Croft'! One once-lovely old cottage looks like a brutally 'made-over' old tart, the picture completed by a gleaming Shogun outside. This, I suspect, is not my kind of village.

Time for a walk: Knacker's Hole Lane runs along the border just south of the village, and I recalled that this intriguing name crops up in various places around the West Country, including one on the Quantocks and another near Tiverton. 'Knackers', of course, is a colloquial name for testicles and, in the past tense, is a term used to describe extreme fatigue. More relevantly, perhaps, the ancient profession of 'knacker' refers to those who dispose of the carcasses of dead or decrepit livestock, but where the 'Hole' bit comes from is unclear. Perhaps the aftermath of the business, ie. rendering fat and burning bones etc., and the accompanying stench, caused the knackers' yards to be confined to out-of-the-way valleys or 'holes'? The latter explanation would certainly fit the Churchinford site. After about a mile sunk between high 'Devon' banks clothed with bracken and rose-bay and interspersed with ancient oak and ash trees, the lane descends steeply to the River Otter in a narrow, steep-sided valley. This is a lovely spot, now the knacker is long gone, the little river tumbling over a tiny double weir to create a watery roar which belies its modest size.

From here the border continues eastward with no access for us, so we followed the valley up the road to the north before turning back to Churchinford and the car. The road we took next across the bleak plateau follows the border closely, crossing the B3170 at Robin Hood's Butts which is, in fact, a group of four or five Bronze Age barrows. The connection with Robin Hood is yet another mystery: it is hard to imagine that the bold Robin ever used this area for shooting practice as he was, after all, supposed to be a Northerner, and I can find no reference to his ever visiting Somerset. It is odd, though, that an 18th century folly near Bridgwater also bears his name, so who knows? Perhaps this worthy scourge of the wicked Normans was a Somerset man after all.

We rejoined the border at the eastern end of the village of Bishopswood, which appears to be an elongated version of Churchinford, so I will refrain from further comment.   The border turns sharply south at this point and it is here that we abandoned the quest for the day and where the next stage will begin. To this end we strolled around to locate the beginning of the south-bound footpath just on the Somerset side following the River Yarty and, having done so, resisted the temptation of the Candlelight Inn and headed for home.

Bishopswood to Tatworth

With Fraser

Liisa, our chauffeuse of the day, deposited us outside the Candlelight Inn at Bishopswood alas, at ten o'clock in the morning, too early for a drink. As we girded our loins for the day's trek I found I had somehow forgotten to bring Roxie's lead, so I ungirded a little by removing my belt to serve as a substitute. At this point a charming lady with an enthusiastic labrador came over to say hello to Roxie and, seeing my ungirded predicament, kindly offered the loan of a lead for the day. As this is a one-way trip with little likelihood of return in the foreseeable future I was forced to decline, but this 'brief encounter' caused me to revise my previously expressed, perhaps harsh, impression of Bishopswood. ("A perfect example of how things happen to you", I heard Fraser murmur in the background. I've no idea what he meant.)

A little way down the lane we found the required footpath running south in close parallel to the border and wrestled our way through an infrequently-used rusty gate into the fields. As is usual in these parts the way-marking is cursory or absent, but we made our way across a couple of sloping fields following the map before turning east, leaving the border which follows the River Yarty continuing south. Trudging up the hill and through a patch of woodland, we came into an open field where I heard, "Well, that was a surprise". I turned to see Fraser, a master of gentle understatement, up to his ankles in black mud in the gateway I had just negotiated, clearly with rather more caution than he. I reminded him that this is still the Blackdowns, where such surprises abound. After admiring a few handsome, purple Greater Knapweed flowers in the meadow, we crossed the field and emerged triumphant onto the A303 with an overgrown stile on the opposite side marking our next footpath.

The dog-unfriendly stile required a bit of 'adjustment' with the boot before Roxie could wriggle through. Then we ascended a couple of gently sloping fields, negotiated a deserted corral made of corrugated iron, rusty hurdles and baler twine, and found ourselves, as predicted, on the little-used tarmac of Giant's Grave road. The name may refer to some ancient burial mounds long ago vanished under the plough, but no trace of the giant remains. The view over the wooded Yarty valley into Devon was a delight as we followed the 220m contour southwards before descending towards the border at Newhaven. The road passes between a farmhouse and its accompanying buildings where Fraser spotted a hand-written sign, taped to the rather elaborate letter-box, instructing the postman to put parcels in the shed "oposit": A commendable economy of both letters and ink. We decided to get off the tarmac and cut a corner, so we diverted onto a bridleway and stopped for a coffee break at the top of another steep valley looking east over the canopy of the woods toward Whitestaunton.

Suitably refreshed we turned into a deep, sunken bridleway. We paused at a rustling and scrabbling in the flail-cropped hedge, and a young roe deer, as startled as we were, appeared alongside us at the top of the bank. Instead of making a rapid getaway whence it came the little deer leapt into the lane a few feet ahead of us before scrambling up the bank on the other side and away into the wood. Roxie tested the improvised belt/lead to the full as she launched herself in pursuit, but both belt and grip held firm and she subsided into grumbling acceptance of the unwelcome restraint. I had only just recovered my composure when she leapt forward again, this time in pursuit of a *cat*, which surely had no business being out there in the wilds. I resisted the temptation, and hung on to the lead/belt, and as the cat disappeared through the hedge and Roxie lost interest we descended a long, sweeping field to join the road to Howley.

A howling flail cutter courteously pulled over to allow us to climb the hill, sticking to the road and avoiding a minor short-cut through a farmyard. I have been told that proposed diversions of these ridiculous through-the-yard footpaths are often opposed 'on principle' by various sanctimonious walking groups who should be ashamed of themselves and of their dopey 'principles'. They should be made to wade through the muckiest of farmyards for all eternity, closely attended by justly irate collies in the guise of Cerberus. Who on earth wants to walk through someone's mucky, collie-defended yard, spooking livestock and unnecessarily upsetting the farmer, when an alternative could easily be provided? Well?

At the top of the hill we entered the hamlet of Howley and stopped to chat with a friendly resident applying a hoe to his pretty front garden next to the road. This stalwart countryman built this and the adjacent bungalows fifty years ago and has supplied himself and his neighbours with water from his borehole, for free, for the last half-century. He told us that he grew up in Yarcombe, a couple of miles across the border in Devon, then moved to the village of Marsh when he was married, before settling here in the 1960's. The little hamlet still retains many of the original inhabitants and their offspring and boasts a real sense of community so often lacking in the rural 'dormitories' of today. Our worthy informant is 87 years old, though he would pass for at least ten years younger, and cheerfully assured us that he makes a point of drinking a glass of cider every day. "At least one", he added, with a wink. The pub down the road would be open, he assured us, and would certainly have some decent cider for us so, with no further delay, we bade him farewell and strolled down the road to the Howley Tavern to seek the elixir of life.

This ancient country inn afforded us, including Roxie, a warm welcome, the atmosphere being marred only by a couple of determined technicians repairing the pool table with a percussive staple gun which might well be a product of Mr Kalashnikov's factory. A pint of Sheppey's is acceptable even under fire, but we tarried no longer than necessary before returning to the trail. Back on the road we could hardly fail to notice a less than lovely barn conversion opposite, bearing a name plate declaring it to be 'Pooh Corner'. What can you say? Without the 'h' it might make some sense.

The footpath from Howley, closely parallel to the border, commences unavoidably through a farmyard where Roxie made a more or less peaceable encounter with the resident collie and where the lady of the farm kindly directed us through the mire. We followed the contour across open fields, once again without much discernible way-marking, crossing the border then heading downhill towards the A30, where we realised that the magnetic pull of Somerset had kept us closer to the border than intended and that we had inadvertently trespassed. Sneaking undetected through an industrial-scale farmyard we hit the road opposite a roaring feed mill belonging to Crawley Farm. This is a little further east than intended so, to avoid a hike along the busy and unpavemented main road, we crossed back into Somerset and took a meandering lane through dense, wild woodland reminiscent of Tolkein, hopefully in the direction of Mounter's Hill

After a brief, belated lunch stop on a grassy bank in the wood we broke out into open fields. Aware that the afternoon was wearing on apace we cut the corner where the border turns sharply east and took the road to Linnington. The footpath marked as Castle Wood Lane on the map looked distinctly unpromising, so we stayed with the road to the border down a steep, wooded hill to the intriguingly-named Shaggs Flood, a pretty house in the bottom of the valley. The road ends abruptly on the border, so we took to a track climbing through more woodland into Devon, then onto one of numerous footpaths or animal tracks leading south-eastwards through what had become a boggy birch wood. Pushing through a gap in a hedge we found ourselves in what appeared to be someone's garden and, indeed, so it was, complete with bee-hives, where the affable resident couple assured us that this is the Right of Way we rather hoped we were on. The lady of the house informed us, quite firmly, that there is nothing wrong with the way-marking in East Devon - it is in South Somerset, to our shame, where such things are neglected - and, after admiring Roxie, she directed us on our way to the aptly-named Cotley Wash. Here the road fords the stream which marks the border, and Fraser took great delight in standing with one foot on each side, a position he had aspired to all day and which was, at last, clearly discernible.

We climbed out of the valley up a steep lane which follows the border, Fraser happily straddling the imaginary line along the middle as we walked. At the top, as we paused at a junction, a huge 4x4 stopped and the charming lady driver asked if we were lost. (Did we really look lost?) She kindly offered us more or less incomprehensible directions which, we hoped, confirmed our intention to continue eastwards along the border on a deep-set lane which crosses and recrosses to and from Devon before emerging at Burridge Cross. We had crossed and re-crossed the border so many times today that I'd lost count.

After a final brief sortie into Devon we re-entered Somerset and left the border on a bridleway across big, open fields towards Tatworth. A comely young lady with a nice pair of labradors pounded past us, pausing briefly to allow the friendlier of the two to offer canine greetings, and for her, the young lady that is, to assure us that Tatworth lay straight ahead. The last lap took us into a deep lane lined with Hazel and big Ash trees and surfaced with lumps of loose chert on grey clay. This is not the easiest of walking for man or dog, but it was downhill and, we earnestly hoped, near the end of today's trail, so there were no complaints.

The Hazel tunnel spat us out onto the roaring A358 which we crossed to take up our position at the bus stop opposite the impressive St John the Evangelist church at Tatworth. As the bus appeared around the corner, right on cue, Fraser was heard to murmur, "Praise the Lord", an appropriate sentiment here in the shadow of St John's, and one which I endorsed most heartily at the end of another long but glorious day on the border trail.

Interlude 4

Big Cats

There's been a lot of talk about 'big cats' roaming around the countryside, and this part of the world seems particularly blessed. We've had the Beast of Exmoor, of course, and then down the road a bit there's the Beast of Bodmin, to name just a couple. My own patch, the Quantocks, hasn't got away scot-free either. We've had the odd panther and puma, and maybe a lynx or two over the years - apparently. It's a pity Quantock doesn't begin with a 'B', or they'd have been Beasts too, I suppose.

Anyway, I get out and about quite a bit, what with working and wandering about with the dog and so on, and I've only seen three up till now. The first was on the Brendons a few years back when the Beast of Exmoor was all the rage. I was living in an old farmhouse that was being 'done up', and the builders swore they'd seen a big, black cat just across the valley only about a quarter of a mile away. "If only we'd had some binoculars or a telephoto," they said.

A couple of months later, with the builders long gone, I was pottering about in the garden when I looked across to the fields on the other side of the valley. There were a few sheep down near the bottom and, at the top, about 100 yards from the sheep, a bloody great black cat was stalking along the hedge.   Allowing for perspective and all that it looked about the same size as the sheep, but sort of cat-shaped. I got the binoculars. It was a cat all right but, even with the binoculars and the sheep in the foreground, it was hard to tell just *how* big it was. I called the dog and we took off down to the valley bottom and up the other side. It only took a couple of minutes. When we got into the sheep field there was no sign of the cat, so we walked up to the far corner, nice and steady, and started moving along the hedge where the Beast had been.

Now you might be thinking that that was a bit foolhardy, so I ought to tell you I'd done a few years in Africa a while back, and I know that leopards and the like will usually run away unless they're *very* hungry. And that's not too likely with all those sheep about, is it? Anyway, we went on along the hedge, keeping our eyes open, when the dog perked up all of a sudden and took off on an angle away from the hedge. He curved round, going like a good 'un, and went into the hedge bottom about 20 yards away like he was after a rabbit.

It was lucky for the cat that there was an old oak growing out of the hedge just along there. It shot up the trunk like something out of a cartoon and stood on the bottom branch with his tail in the air and his fur all sticking up like a hedgehog. It was a bloody moggy, of course. A fair-sized one right enough, but I still can't see how I could have thought it was a panther. It just goes to show. I've seen plenty of black cats in my time, all shapes and sizes, and more than a couple of real leopards on their home ground, so how I could've thought that moggy was a panther beats me. Yes. It just goes to show.

The second 'big cat' was a bit scarier, in a way. Same farm house. I was heading for the bathroom one morning and just as I passed the tall, narrow window on the landing, I saw a sheep fair flying across the field of view like it had the devil on its tail. I couldn't see that much out of the narrow window, but I did see the sheep crash into the stock fence and bounce off like a kid off a trampoline. Then, right behind it, as the poor sheep shot out of view, a long, low black animal, going hell for leather, was right on its heels. Now if that was all I'd seen I'd have pretty much sworn that the black streak was a cat, about the same size as the sheep but longer and lower - and faster. I sprinted back to the bedroom to get a better view. Whoever had so-called 'trained' that collie - yes, the 'beast' was a collie - needed seeing to. That stray sheep could've had a heart attack, poor beggar. Surprising, to say the least, that I could have mistaken that dog for a big cat. To be fair, though, next time you see a collie going flat out you'll maybe see why.

The third one was only a couple of years ago, right here, just under the Quantocks. We were coming back from a good walk early one autumn morning, the old dog trotting ahead as usual. All of a sudden, he dropped on his belly, ears and hackles well up. He was part German Shepherd, part collie and part lurcher was old George, and a marvellous dog. Gone on now, sad to say. Anyway, the next second, he was up and off at full pelt. Then I saw what he'd seen. A bloody great black 'cat' flat on his belly in the stubble about 50 yards away and facing towards us.

"Christ," I thought, "this is it." Old George was one hell of a dog, but I wasn't sure how he'd shape up against a real live panther. I'd only galloped a few yards in pursuit when George skidded to a halt in front of the big black job, which rolled over on its back and waved its legs in the air. It was a bloody labrador. Now I have to admit old George had a bit of a reputation, and the local dogs knew full well he wasn't to be messed with. The poor old lab had flattened down ready to pounce before he realised what was coming. When he saw who it was he did the sensible thing and surrendered. Still, until he rolled over, that long black shape, down flat and ready to spring, had me fooled for a minute, despite my previous 'cat' experiences. Just goes to show.

And only last year, a neighbour of mine reckoned he saw a big orange job come flying out of a hedge just up the track there and shoot off into the copse. He said he thought it was a puma or cougar or something. Maybe a lynx. Well, if that was a puma or whatever, and not that nasty Rhodesian Ridgeback that used to live down the road, then I'm a kangaroo. What do you think?

Until some reputable soul comes up with some real evidence, I think we can sleep more of less safely in our beds, at least in Somerset.

The Deep South

Crewkerne Turning to North Perrott

and on to Yeovil

With Geoff

Heading for Somerset's Deep South on the bus from Taunton we passed swiftly through Chard and on to the border with Devon at Crewkerne Turning. The obliging driver kindly dropped us off right on the border, where we turned east on a footpath to Chilson. The most southerly point in Somerset is about half a mile to the south but there is no public access, so from Chilson we took another footpath north-east parallel to the border, following the course of the meandering River Axe. (This is one of two rivers of the same name in Somerset.   This one rises in Dorset and meets the sea near Sidmouth in Devon while the other, exclusive to Somerset, rises in the Mendip Hills and runs westwards to the Bristol Channel.)

This is open, rolling country over broad grass fields, and here we encountered the first of many troublesome stiles. Roxie is reluctant to jump these things, though they are well within her capability, preferring to wriggle and scrabble under the bottom bar in an awkward and inelegant fashion. The paths are not well marked and, apparently, little used, but we managed to find our way to the railway crossing and followed the track alongside the river which is heavily flanked by swathes of Himalayan Balsam.   This big, handsome plant with its pink snap-dragon flowers and intriguing wriggling seed pods was a favourite of my childhood along the Avon, but its incursive habit now ensures its persecution by conservationists and water-men alike. But here it's winning.

The path follows the foot of the railway embankment on our left while on our right an imposing chain-link fence separated us from the concrete bulk of a murmuring sewage-treatment plant followed, somewhat incongruously, by a huge dairy-processing factory. This odd juxtaposition caused us to wonder if either one services the other in some mysterious way: Is it fanciful to imagine the heat from the sewage plant powering the milk factory while the waste from the factory conveniently slips into the sewage facility next door?   It seems odd, otherwise, that sewage and food-processing should be such close neighbours.

We turned east and crossed the Axe over a small road bridge and made our first incursion into Dorset, the second-loveliest county in England.   After a mile or so along the quiet road we turned off northward to rejoin the river and the border on the rather inappropriately named Liberty Trail.   This traces the route supposedly taken by some supporters of the Duke of Monmouth to join his rebel army at Lyme Regis in 1665, resulting in a fate which was a far cry from Liberty. This ill-fated campaign marks some of the darkest days in Somerset's history, when Monmouth attempted to dislodge the Catholic James II with an army of naturally rebellious but ill-equipped and untrained Westcountrymen. We paused to wonder what drove hundreds of Somerset men, mostly artisans and farm-workers, to throw away their lives for a cause which could only replace one autocratic clown with another.   Surely not just sectarianism?   Whatever the reason, the brutal retribution which followed the dithering Monmouth's failure lurks still in the folk-memory of the region and, perhaps, explains the lack of enthusiasm for monarchy remaining to this day in much of the Westcountry. But enough of that, before I start sharpening my bill-hook.

Crossing the border back into Somerset over a footbridge we followed the river through pretty meadows and caught a view of the handsome Forde Abbey on the Dorset side. In the 14th century the Abbey owned 30,000 acres of land, much of it in Somerset, but the lot was appropriated by Henry VIII as part of the old reprobate's Dissolution programme in 1539. Since then it has passed through numerous hands, some more responsible than others, and is now a privately-owned tourist attraction.

We pressed on along this pretty valley, passing through small groups of Devon Red cattle, and re-crossed the railway at the hamlet of Ammerham. Still on the Liberty Trail, four or five more small fields with tricksy stiles took us to the village of Winsham just a couple of hundred yards north of the border, and here we earnestly hoped to find a pub. Alas, it was a Monday, and The Bell at Winsham is closed on Mondays. Disappointed but not entirely dejected we retired to the churchyard of the 13th century St Stephen's for a teetotal picnic, sitting on a grand sarcophagus whose inscription has long been eroded beyond deciphering. This is a delightfully peaceful spot in the shadow of the ancient tower, with swallows skimming around the grotesques adorning the corners. Only the one which carries the water from the roof is a true gargoyle and is distinguished by the pipe emerging from its mouth. The others, in place for the sake of architectural balance, are known as chimera or, according to some authorities, as 'hunky punks' in local dialect, though I have never heard the term used by anyone resembling a 'local'. Here they appear to represent a frog-like creature, a wolf of sorts and a bloke with a big nose, while the gargoyle itself may be a dragon or similar beast. What these alien carvings have to do with Christianity is a bit of a mystery, though they are pretty ubiquitous on Somerset church towers and surely lend a certain pagan jauntiness to these otherwise reverent sites.

As we took our leave of this pleasant, unpretentious village a little black cat of extreme age and decrepitude barred our way on the pavement, seemingly quite unaware of our presence. Roxie was so amazed by this inadvertent show of defiance that she allowed me to lead her to the other side of the road without protest, shaking her head in disbelief at this geriatric feline audacity.

We rejoined the Liberty Trail continuing eastward, running parallel to the border which is half a mile or so to the south. We were struck once again by the sparsity of population in this part of South Somerset, this perhaps explaining the little-used and neglected state of many of the Rights of Way hereabouts: there's nobody here to use them. There is little in the way of habitation between the widely-spaced farms, and even the rolling pastureland is largely bereft of livestock, the effect of which is a slightly eerie 'Marie Celeste' feel about the place. The Trail descends a steepish, wooded hillside to the hamlet of Wayford, dominated by the imposing Manor which must be of ancient origin as it was rebuilt in the 16th century. Extensively refurbished and extended in the early 20th century, it is still in private ownership and now graciously participates in the National Gardens Scheme.

Still on the Liberty Trail we took to the road for a while, passing under the railway and turning off on a bridleway through Clapton Farm which resembled a monumental agricultural junk-yard. We climbed steeply up over fields littered with an array of rusting machinery and decomposing vehicles which must be worth a fortune in scrap value these days. We followed the contour across the scantily way-marked fields at around 150m with wondrous views to the west over intricately-folded farmland dotted with patches of woodland. Joining the road at Henley Cross we turned south-east, once again parallel to the nearby border, and strolled down the vehicle-free lane to Duck's Field Crossing with sweeping views away to the south into Dorset. From here we abandoned the Liberty Trail in favour of the more direct lane to Misterton, then struck off on a footpath which leads to the A356 in the middle of the village, where the PH symbol on the map had raised our hopes of much needed refreshment.

At 4.30 in the afternoon we were confronted by the White Swan, emblazoned with advertisements for Cedric's Cider, but was this ancient hostelry open? There was no sign of life but, just as we were about to abandon hope, the door opened and the charming lady of the house kindly offered us a 'take-away' pint which we were at liberty to drink in the garden across the road. While we enjoyed an excellent pint of Cedric's best and Roxie refreshed herself from a convenient dog-bowl, the proprietor, presumably Cedric, joined us for a chat about cider, gardening and suchlike weighty matters. If you are ever passing through Misterton you should do yourself a favour and call in for a pint of Cedric's and a slice of their fine apple cake.

Suitably invigorated we took our leave and found the footpath eastwards across the fields where a bunch of assorted bullocks took a keen interest in our progress.   Roxie would rather like to play but, in the interests of safety (whose?) I kept her on the leash and the bullocks followed us closely with a fair bit of hopping and skipping before forming a tight Roman Square formation. Instead of the anticipated charge, the front line lost interest and started grazing, still in close formation, leaving us to pass on in peace. (There are many reported incidents of bullocks, and even heifers, 'harassing' walkers, particularly with dogs, but I have never come across any which couldn't be stopped with a friendly word and a bit of hand-waving.) This is as good a time as any to mention Geoff's beloved walking 'pole' again, the lamented absence of which featured in our Exmoor walk. On this trek it has protruded proudly from his rucksack the whole way, emerging only to be waved at the bullocks. QED.

The course of the footpath was far from clear but we managed to find our way to the ford across the River Parrett, right on the border. I had never realised that the Parrett arose so far south, but I suppose the nearby villages of North and South Perrott offer a clue. At the intriguingly-named Pipplepen Farm we left the border for the day and struck north on the River Parrett Trail to our overnight stop in North Perrott. Over more open grassy fields we crossed the railway again and descended gently to the A3066 and a short hop into the village. The cottages lining the road are all constructed of the beautiful, golden Hamstone so characteristic of this area, and any 'doing-up' has been tasteful and unobtrusive. Despite the 'main' road this place has a good feel about it, and the Manor Arms is not a disappointment - except, perhaps, for the lack of Cedric's cider. The staff are friendly, our rooms were cosy, the food is good and the ale is local. After dinner Roxie was treated to a dish of sausages by the cheery staff, and all was surely well with the world.

After a fine breakfast, it was thanks and goodbye to the Manor Arms. Heading south on a convenient path back to the border, a pack of assorted farm dogs came out to greet us, but one look at the dancing Longdog persuaded them to keep their distance, and we carried on unmolested into the emptiness of South Somerset.

The footpath across gently sloping fields and around the edge of a wood confronted us with more dubious way-marking and dog-unfriendly stiles, but Roxie managed to wriggle through all but one, which required a helping hand in the form of a Howard-style lift. We passed another collection of huge, sprawling farm buildings apparently devoid of livestock, and encountered a field of stunted maize through which the footpath is supposed to pass. Rather than bash through even this miserable crop we skirted it and eventually found our way into Ashland Coppice with the help of Geoff's magic electronic navigator. (Map reference to five digits each way, no less!) The 'coppice' is, in fact, a conifer plantation which had recently been fiercely thinned, leaving the path heavily covered with brash which does nothing for easy walking for man or dog. A quick check of the map revealed that we had just "slipped over the border", to quote my trusty companion who, as an Irishman, knows about these things.

We exited the wood into scrubby brush under a pylon line and joined the Monarch's Way running more or less north/south. This is part of the route supposedly taken by the fugitive Charles II after his defeat by Cromwell's boys at Worcester, running from there to Brighton, from whence the blighter made his escape. There are no Rights of Way along the border from here so we must make a detour, retracing the steps of the 'merry monarch' and crossing back into Somerset heading north across more, I almost said interminable, grasslands. Yet another railway crossing took us to the hamlet of Hardington Marsh, which is actually one huge farm and a few tarted-up cottages, when the previously brooding clouds delivered their goods with a vengeance and we took hasty cover in a handy lean-to garage by the roadside until the torrent abated.

A footpath to the east took us away from the Monarch's Way towards the hamlet of Pendomer, and somewhere along this series of ill-signed paths and nastily overgrown stiles I noticed the absence of my map-reading glasses which a short retracing of steps failed to find. The extended string of grumbling curses accidentally recorded, to my shame, on the dictaphone relates, I think, more to the wretched Rights of Way maintenance in these parts than to the minor inconvenience of the specs-loss. Geoff's glasses were, thankfully, still with us so he was officially sworn-in as Navigator in Chief, which is certainly an improvement on the previous incumbent. Just in time to restore our good humour a pair of pretty, half-grown roe deer nodded at us from an overgrown field, happily for them below Roxie's line of sight.

The next two enormous fields we had to cross were recently down to corn and had been harvested and cultivated to break up the stubble before ploughing, which made for uncomfortable walking for all three of us. Geoff's electronics were again called for to locate the overgrown stile in the hedge separating these two prairies, and it was with some relief that we escaped from this grim arable desert through another vast, unoccupied farmyard and onto the road.

The most notable feature of Pendomer is the 13th century church just visible through the trees. We should, perhaps, have taken the time to take a closer look if for no other reason than that its dedication is to St Roch who, among other distinctions, is the patron saint of dogs. (This honour, apparently, is due to his life being saved by the timely ministrations of a benevolent canine, to which he was quite rightly eternally grateful.) We had little choice here but to turn away from the border for a while in order to skirt the north end of Sutton Bingham reservoir, as its southern end, right on the border, has no way round without making deep incursions into Dorset. At this crucial decision-point Geoff expressed the earnest desire to visit the village of East Coker, only a minor detour to the north. This was not only on account of the possibility of a pub, apparently, but from his wish to see the village made famous by the eponymous (and thoroughly dismal) poem of T.S.Eliot. More significant for a sea-faring man I suspect, is that the village is the birthplace of the 17th century buccaneer William Dampier. This swashbuckling son of Somerset enjoyed a varied career, to say the least, in the manner of the polymath mariners of his time, and is well worth honouring as such, so off we went to East Coker.

Having had enough of South Somerset's dubious footpaths for the moment we opted for the elevated lanes leading north-east, the first of which is lined with truly enormous trees which, I think, must be rare Black Poplars. They are quite magnificent, as are the views to the north and west when we reached the top of the incline before descending gently to rejoin the Monarch's Way along an avenue of ancient oaks crossing Coker Court Park. We were rewarded by an exceptionally pretty village heralded by the lovely 17th century Hamstone almshouses, but we failed to afford them their due attention as we proceeded through the adjacent churchyard with unseemly haste as the time was fast approaching two o'clock and we feared the curse of closing time. Fortunately, the handsome Helyar Arms observes no such nonsense, and we were warmly welcomed while Roxie graciously received her usual admiration.

After an excellent lunch, served by a strikingly elegant landlady, we emerged into bright sunshine and took the quiet lane back to the border via the quaintly-named Pincushion Corner, passed the north-end dam of the reservoir and hit the busy A37 which we crossed with only minor risk to life and limb. Elsford Bridge took us across a pretty little river which must be a tributary of the Yeo, and back into Dorset, if only just. We turned off the road onto a bridleway which follows the border closely on its way northward over undulating farmland, with endless green views to the west. In one of the vast stubble-fields we crossed, a small-baler was at work on the straw, and the driver gave us a cheery wave, suggesting, we hoped, that we were on the right path despite the lack of any useful way-marking. We passed through another huge, deserted farmyard and met the road near the village of Stoford.

The map is quite clear that our next footpath is directly opposite our exit from the bridleway, but it was unmarked and the field-gate was chained and padlocked. Fortunately, the gate-hanging was not the work of a professional so we were able to lift it off its hinges to allow Roxie through. We waded across a field of knee-high clover to join the border and the railway line near Yeovil Junction Station and, again, the course of the footpath is open to debate. We found our way, eventually, under the railway, where a notice warns sternly that the penalty for failing to close the gate is £2! At this point the line of the border on the map disappears in a tangle of railway lines and we can only assume that it follows the curve of the track, odd as that may seem. For want of alternative we took a little-used footpath which climbs steeply northward to join Newton Road on its way to Yeovil. The road was uncomfortably busy so we turned off at the first opportunity then picked up a footpath running parallel to the road through dense woodland with a steep drop to the traffic down below. I was just about to remark on the easiness of this path when we encountered the first of several large, fallen trees barring our way, and a good deal of agility was required from us all to negotiate them without tumbling down the precipice.

We made our exit from the wood with some relief, emerging onto the steep, open parkland of Summerhouse Hill, a green and pleasant 'amenity area' overlooking Yeovil. At the bottom of the hill we crossed a footbridge and found ourselves, without any suburban preamble, at the back of a giant building which might be a warehouse, a sports centre or any other ghastly, anonymous modern prefabrication. Rounding the corner, we stumbled into a pedestrian shopping precinct which, at 5.30 in the afternoon, was deserted except for a few hoodies and loungers-in-doorways, all with cans in hand. After two days walking and with a big lurcher alongside we neither looked nor felt at all out of place, lacking only the cans.

With nearly an hour before our bus was due to leave we located the bus station then looked around for suitable refreshment. The only visible hostelry in this bleak concrete wasteland is an enormous chain-pub with countless entrances and all the charm of a busy charnel-house. We were resigning ourselves to a comfortless wait when Geoff spied the Yeovil Labour Club, with a small neon 'bar' sign in the window, across the road from the bus station. Closer investigation revealed a locked door and a 'No Dogs' sign, so we were sitting disconsolately at one of the tables outside when an elderly couple approached up the steps. "D'you want to go in?" the man asked affably. We explained our predicament, confessed to being non-members (though Geoff's wife is a Party member!) and hoped for the best. This friendly chap regretted the no-dog rule but invited us to get a drink which we could enjoy where we were on the terrace. The man is a hero and a saviour. After a couple of minutes Geoff returned in triumph bearing a couple of pints of decent cider, and my previously held opinions of Yeovil (and the Labour Party) were rapidly revised.

We were hardly into the pints when another man came out onto the terrace for a cigarette, noticed Roxie stretched out under the table and promptly trotted off to fill a dog bowl for her. Yeovil is definitely a good place after all. When he returned we talked about our border walk and he told us that his golf club, just down the road, spans the county boundary, one hole having the tee in Somerset and the pin over the river in Dorset. Golf sans frontiers.

After more fraternal and interesting chat, we bade our golfing friend farewell and scampered back to the bus station. The bus rolled in, we flashed our passes and sat back to enjoy the delights of the Somerset lowlands on the way back to Taunton. Roxie stretched out languorously across the back seat and no-one seemed to mind. This was a long and sometimes taxing hike across Somerset's Deep South but, obscure footpaths and lost glasses notwithstanding, as full of interest and delights as ever.

Interlude 5

Cider

Somerset is cider and cider is Somerset. It's true they have a decent shot at it in Hereford … pause for digression: I'm ashamed to say that the first time I was ever seriously drunk on cider was in Hereford. In mitigation, I was about 10 years old and the proud cox of a local rowing club. My crew was knocked out in the first heat of the regatta at Hereford, but our other crew fought their way through to the final. What was my crew to do all day but frequent the beer tent? Each time a round was brought in, their disconsolate cox was given half a pint of cider. Nowadays such irresponsible behaviour would be considered reprehensible if not illegal, but then …

As we made our way home in our customised 1950's hearse (perfect for carrying boats and crew) my perception of the world was altered substantially and I threw up heartily out of the back doors as we trundled along. When we got home my ever-tolerant parents received their semi-comatose son with their usual equanimity. My love affair with cider continues to this day.

Where was I? Ah yes, cider. As well as Hereford, some other regions ferment a few apples now and again. Devon, apparently, has a go, as does Norfolk, wherever that is. There are even rumours that the French have a drop left over from Calvados production but, for the true cider aficionado, it has to be Somerset.

Having made such a bold claim, even I have to admit that not <u>all</u> Somerset cider is wonderful. Most, yes, but not quite all. I was driving up towards Weston-super-Mare a while ago when I spotted a roadside sign I'd never noticed before: 'Champion Cider' or somesuch. The farmyard looked a bit ratty sure enough, but that doesn't mean much so I pulled in, resolved to give this discovery a try. I was greeted by a young lady, six feet tall and built like a bullock, who directed me round the back to the cider barn. After a few minutes the old chap, presumably her father, turned up and unlocked the creaking old door. In the gloom of the interior a couple of rows of huge barrels shared the space with a tangle of dust-covered agricultural history.

"We got medium and dry," he announced. "Do 'ee want to try 'em?"

I told him I usually favoured dry, but I'd be grateful to try both. He was happy to oblige, and while he was drawing off a couple of samples he proudly informed me that his family had been making cider here for three generations. Guessing that the old boy was in his sixties, that would carry their cider-making pedigree back to the 19th century. Impressive.

As I'd established my credentials as more or less 'local' he went on to describe some of the "vis'tors" (holiday makers) who called in.

"D'you know," he said, "some buggers come in t'other day and asked for a sample, like. The bloke said t'was all right, but his missus, this is true mind, said t'was only good for putting on chips! Cheeky cow."

By this time, I'd managed to force down my throat the sample of what tasted like neat nail-varnish remover. Eyes watering, I moved on to the 'medium'. This was rather more subtle, the acetone being tempered with battery acid. I bought half a gallon of the latter, out of politeness, and made my getaway before the bullock came back.

Most less-than-perfect cider can be rendered palatable by the ancient process of mulling. The addition of a stick of cinnamon, a few cloves, a scrape of nutmeg and a handful of sugar usually does the trick when gently heated. Not this one. It needed half a bottle of brandy to bring this vicious potion up to the mark.

Another salutary tale might act as a warning to vis'tors. A few years ago, I attended a local village fete on the Brendons. I was with some more or less civilised friends so I was probably less obviously local than usual when I checked out the beer tent.

"Got any decent cider?" I asked the ruddy-faced barman.

He gave me an appraising look. "Oh ah," he said, slyly, "we got some proper stuff."

He ran off a pint from an unmarked plastic barrel at the back of the tent and set it down on the trestle table. "That'll be two quid."

I took a sip of the nasty looking orange liquid and put the plastic 'glass' back on the counter. "Tell you what," I said, pleasantly, "*you* drink a pint of that poisonous rat's piss and I'll pay for both of 'em. Otherwise you know what you can do with 'n."

He grinned, almost sheepishly. "Sorry, mate," he said. "I thought you were, y'know, not from round here, like. Want a pint of Sheppey's ?"

Which is not to condemn all small-scale producers. Far from it. All you have to do is find them. For example, on the Taunton side of the Levels is a modest farm which produces excellent cider in the traditional way year after year. And this particular apple nectar has the advantage of being made and dispensed by the prettiest cider-maid in Somerset, accompanied by her dad, a genial and knowledgeable countryman with a host of cider-making tales. My frequent visits to Parsonage Farm near Westlyng are always an education and a delight. Try it.

Moving up a league, so to speak, we come to the three or four large-scale producers. These have all developed from traditional 'farm house' methods but have scaled up in recent times to meet an ever-increasing demand. This sounds ominous, but I can truly say that those I occasionally frequent still manage to produce acceptable draught ciders despite the modernisation. A couple of them, at least, also knock out a range of bottled ciders which aren't at all bad, though I draw the line at adulteration with blackberries and the like. Still, townies and 'foreigners' seem to enjoy them, so good luck to them.

Altogether, there are Somerset ciders to suit pretty much every taste, but please don't equate our County's trademark beverage with the nasty, gassy stuff which emerges from shiny dispensers in all too many pubs, even in Somerset. They should be ashamed of themselves.

Brendon Two Gates.

More high Exmoor.

Bridge over the River Barle at Withypool

'Salmon trap' on the Barle.

Exmoor sheep with attitude.

'Pyramids' at Foxcote. Any ideas?

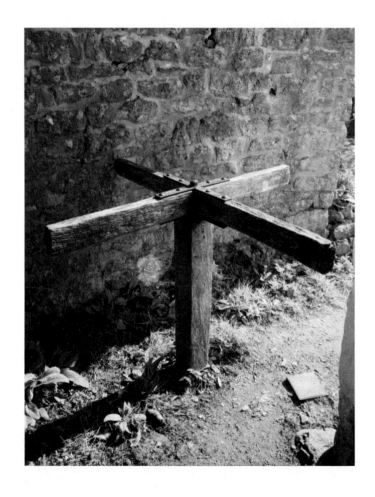

Church path 'turnstile' at Cucklington.

Stile demolition at Huish House.

Jack and Jill at Kilmersdon

Stone circle near Harptree Hill. Not quite as old as Stonehenge.

The Far East

Yeovil to Wincanton

With Geoff

We boarded an early bus from Taunton to Yeovil and seemed to float across the magically misty Levels, with a flock of geese in silhouette against the silver disc of the sun. The back seat was occupied, so Roxie stretched out on the floor with a grumpy sigh, determined to cause as much obstruction as possible while our tolerant fellow passengers scrambled around her without complaint.

Arriving in Yeovil we paused for a guilty coffee as the sun broke through and lit up what now appeared as a spacious square in a relatively pleasant shopping precinct. "A bit different from last time," Geoff remarked, as we observed the cheery passers-by and recalled the crepuscular hoodies and hoodlums lurking around on our last visit. Could this really be the same place?

Time to go. We left the town centre and headed for the border through Yeovil's anonymous north-east suburbs, with Roxie's nose in hyper-sniff mode as she checked out the myriad of novel dog smells. The first cat of the day provoked the usual flurry of activity, but the wretched feline wisely froze, and the hunter's interest quickly waned. Moving targets are much more exciting.

One thing to be said in favour of Yeovil is that it doesn't sprawl, and we left the town abruptly on Primrose Lane between big, open fields towards Mudford, where we crossed the river Yeo at Mudford Bridge and turned south-east on the Monarch's Way into Dorset. The beautiful yellow stone of the cottages and barns in the village of Adber shone through the gentle drizzle, but our delight in the place was somewhat tempered by finding the footpath back over the border comprehensively blocked by a locked gate and a fenced-in stable yard. How do they get away with it? It is of little comfort that rights of way violations of this sort are not endemic only to Somerset but, with little choice other than gate-shattering vandalism, we retraced our steps and rejoined the lane which follows the border south and then east.

This stretch of the border, and some others we have encountered, is marked by numerous sharp changes of direction which make the proverbial dog's hind leg seem as straight as a billiard cue. I can only imagine that these odd twists and turns, sometimes following water courses, contours or field boundaries but often apparently at random, mark the boundaries of the old Saxon fiefdoms which were later handed over in great chunks to the Norman Invader's henchmen.

At this point we decided to cut across one of these incursions of Dorset and continue to Sandford Orcas, the latter name of which probably derives from a corruption of the name of one of the early Norman bandits and not, reasonably enough, from the killer whales. It may be that our decision was influenced by the presence of the pub symbol on the map but, if so, we were to be disappointed. Once again, the inn is closed on Mondays and today is, of course, Monday. Is this the custom in this part of the world, or is it a conspiracy? I was sorely piqued, as this looked like the sort of place which might have harboured some good cider despite being in Dorset, but Geoff was handsomely magnanimous and stoical as ever, recalling with remarkable good humour the similar let-down in East Coker back in August.

We rejoined the border at Staffords Green and looked north across some glorious rolling country to the imposing hump of Cadbury Castle standing out from the surrounding steep scarps characteristic of this part of the County. The 'castle' is, in fact, the site of a Bronze Age hill fort with a long and heroic history, with evidence of settlement from Neolithic times continuing to post-Roman occupation. While archaeological opinions differ, it seems likely that its colourful past includes a spirited and prolonged resistance to Vespasian's legions (in the manner of Asterix in Gaul?) and perhaps, a little later, as the site of Arthur's Camelot.

 We pressed on, following the border eastwards before taking the 'wrong' bridleway under Poyntington Down and straying inadvertently back into Dorset along a boggy, Exmoor-like valley following a meandering stream: the source of the River Yeo, no less. We exchanged pleasantries with a herd of pretty ponies complete with colourful coats and braided forelocks, then climbed out of the valley to rejoin the border on a bridleway running south along the top of a steep scarp. Down below we spotted a solitary figure in the middle of a vast brassica field, and we debated whether this was a man or a scarecrow. Doubt was dispelled as he began to crawl about among the crop, our conclusion being that he was either setting up or sampling from insect traps used to identify optimum spraying times. We had already watched a 100ft spraying rig in action earlier in the day, and we were bound to lament the further poisoning of the countryside, no matter how efficiently targeted.

A hazy sun was with us again, and the gold-tinged views to the west were glorious indeed. Being on top of the ridge, the course of the path was pretty obvious, which was fortunate as the way-marking, as usual in these parts, was lacking. At the southern end of the ridge the bridleway leaves the border for another brief incursion into Dorset via Donkey Lane and, like the rest of this stretch of bridleway, the lane was overgrown, bramble-ridden and little-used, and had certainly seen no donkeys for some time. Once again, the border itself became inaccessible, but a diversion through Milborne Port, checking out the pubs for later, took us back to the west side of the 'Milborne Port Bulge' just south of the little town.   An easy, uneventful stroll down the Goathill Road led to the most southerly point of the 'pedicle' where we turned northwards and followed the border up the east side of the bulge on a bridleway through a boggy but beautiful mature deciduous wood.

As we entered the wood Roxie snapped into Full Alert, and in a dip in the trail about fifty yards ahead we could see why: Two roe deer, one all black, were browsing happily on the shrubbery. Luckily the sloping ground obscured them from her view if not from her nose, so we distracted her with intelligent conversation while slowly advancing, causing the little dryads, only mildly alarmed, to skip off into the boggy thickets blissfully unaware of the magnitude of the potential danger. As we reached the browsing spot the Longdog's nose connected with the scent, and she reared up like a giant meerkat, scanning the undergrowth for the vanished prey. Thwarted, she pranced ahead on tip-toes with the life-saving lead at full stretch until the excitement had subsided. As we neared the end of the wood the light was fading, but the fallen beech leaves were glowing orange and gold as we negotiated the final stile and crossed a couple of fields to hit the A30 at Crendle Corner.

Thankfully this busy road is blessed with a functional pavement at the point where we left the border to head for Milborne Port on the last leg of today's trek. During our earlier sortie into the town Geoff had cunningly checked out the timetable and had calculated (he is a mathematician, after all) that the bus for Sherborne should be passing shortly. Sure enough and right on cue the bus appeared behind us, so we smartly crossed the road into a convenient lay-by and attempted to flag it down. Alas, the bastard roared past without so much as a blink, leaving us to trudge on into Milborne Port where we took refuge in the Tippling Philosopher.   Geoff made the customary dog-reconnaissance and was assured she would be welcome "as long as she's quiet". ("I've got a Rottweiler out the back," the amiable landlord told him, though the significance of this information was not entirely clear.) The gentle buzz of rural conversation and a pint of Cheddar Valley Red soon restored our good humour, so we ceased cursing the bus-driver (who was surely only abiding by the rules, after all) and summoned a taxi.

It is a shame if not an outright disgrace that I had been unable to find any dog-friendly accommodation in Milborne Port, forcing us to resort to a night over the border in Sherborne. There we found that their dog-friendliness amounted to confining the poor hound to my room, so after dinner we repaired to a pub down the road where they welcomed a Longdog but were lacking in decent cider. So much for Dorset.

After a rather posh breakfast and a provisioning trip to the supermarket, we waited for our taxi on the corner of a junction which provided entertainment in the form of several near-misses in just a few minutes. Whether these close encounters were due to the nature of the junction or to the advanced age of the majority of Sherborne drivers is not clear. Our cheery, relatively youthful driver transported us back over the border to the safety of Somerset. The sun came out and we set off on a footpath across a couple of open fields, the entertainment here being provided by a string of elegant race-horses exercising on a curving, sandy gallop.

We climbed the first steep, wooded ridge of the day and joined the border along a bridleway marked on the map as The Old Road once, apparently, the main highway to London but now no more than a rutted track. On our right a high fence confined a herd of fifty or so red deer, complete with a couple of magnificent ten-point stags. On my beloved Quantock Hills the wild stags would be bawling and brawling at this time of year, but these two noble specimens seemed content to share the harem, and even to tolerate the presence of a couple of young stags in their midst. Perhaps this is one consequence of domestication, never a desirable state. The sunken track we were on concealed them from Roxie's view, so she loped along in blissful ignorance, the breeze carrying their scent away out of range of her olfactory apparatus.

Crossing the A30 we turned south along the border atop another wooded ridge where, despite the clear bridleway marker, the track soon deteriorated after we passed a couple of nasty, incongruous telephone masts, one unconvincingly disguised as a pine tree. The views from these ridges are consistently vast and beautiful, and we paused to acknowledge that the heavy hand of agri-business has touched the land but lightly here. Following the border, we turned eastward along a quiet tarmac lane flanked by a magnificent stone wall, about ten feet high, on the Dorset side. This is believed to have been built early in the 18th century to extend and enclose the parkland attached to the manor at Stalbridge and would certainly have served to obstruct the view from the Somersetians of the time. I marvelled once again at our ancestors' reluctance to follow the example of the French Revolution.

After about a mile the wall ends near the A357 which we crossed and continued to follow the border along Landshire Lane for another mile or so before turning north, cutting across another county protuberance which contains a sprawling trading estate occupying the site of what once was Henstridge Airfield. Only one private runway remains of what was a significant training base in WWII, the rest being swallowed up by factories and warehouses of indeterminate sorts. The whole area is high and flat, as we might expect of a former airfield, and this, along with the unaccustomed traffic and howling wind, encouraged a speedy traverse of this rather unlovely place. Roxie's lowered head and grumpy expression indicated that she was as anxious to be out of there as we were.

We hit the A30 at Bow Bridge, crossed it and attempted to rejoin the border as it follows Bow Brook northwards. The footpath, clearly marked on the map, was conspicuously unmarked on the ground and, just to keep things interesting, the field boundaries were not quite as they once were and the going underfoot was like a swamp. In the course of recent stream dredging a huge tree had been ripped out and now lay forlorn in the bog in a tangle of shattered branches. These provided a dry seat and shelter from the ever-present wind, so we clambered aboard for a lunch break. Unable to find a dry spot to lie down, Roxie leant disconsolately against a broken branch and received her share of the sandwiches with little grace.

As we waded out of our lunchtime haven a curious roe deer popped out of the hedge, quickly realised the danger and made off at speed as Roxie pranced on the end of the lead in frustration. After calming her down we abandoned the attempt to find the footpath and cut across the fields to Park Lane, thus avoiding the extensive buildings of Mohuns Park. The name is notorious in West Somerset, the Mohuns being the first recipients of Dunster Castle and its surrounding estates when William the Norman was dishing out the goodies in the 11th century. They were not popular among the natives, with the third incumbent being known as the Scourge of Somerset on account of his rather heavy-handed stewardship, so we felt well justified in giving this place a wide berth, just in case.

After another brief incursion into Dorset we turned back into Somerset on a surprisingly busy B road. Here, Roxie's ever-enquiring nose detected a dead otter on the verge, and we lamented the passing of this lovely creature, doubtless under the wheels of an unknowing vehicle. Our experiences with the tricksy, unmarked, unwalked footpaths around here persuaded us to run the gauntlet of the traffic for another half mile along the road before we took a quiet lane east through more flat, open fields. It occurred to us that, with the exception of the jockeys and distant insect-gatherer, we had not seen a single soul outside the confines of a vehicle since we left Milborne Port hours before.

A series of dog-legs took us to the village of Cucklington, perched on a steep, west-facing ridge about a mile west of the border. This is a thoroughly picturesque little place with breath-taking views over the vale, so it came as no surprise that the average property price over the last five years is around half a million pounds! I wonder how many 'locals' live here.   At the north end of the village we circumnavigated the 13th century church of St Lawrence by way of a footpath guarded by an ancient wooden turnstile contraption of a type I have never encountered before. The path leads through the well-kept churchyard then to the top of a steep scarp where the howling wind caught us again, while the late afternoon sun added touches of gold to the glorious, sparsely-populated panorama below.

From the ridge path we negotiated a stile onto a 'restricted byway'. This designation was introduced in 2006 when the former 'byways open to all traffic' (BOATs), and 'roads used as public paths' (RUPPs) were closed to motorised vehicles, much to the chagrin of 'off-road' enthusiasts and the delight of walkers, cyclists and horse-riders. This track leads to the magnificent 17th century golden-stone edifice of Clapton Farm, complete with extensive matching outbuildings which appeared to straddle the footpath. Once again, we could find no way-markers and not a living soul to ask the way, so we played safe and took a lane leading back towards the border and the B3081. We passed under the roaring A303 and began the last lap along an unclassified road which, to our initial surprise, was carrying far more traffic than made any sense - until, that is, we realised that this 'little' road is the main route out of Wincanton to join the A303. With the sun low in our eyes and a very narrow verge, this made for a thoroughly unhealthy trek into the on-coming traffic. The tiring Roxie needed continuous encouragement to keep going in the face of the repeated close encounters, but she plodded on stoically until we reached the safety of the Hunters' Lodge. This is a typical road-house, with a no-dogs rule and a lack of decent cider, but the affable barman was informative about the marketing ploys of the big pseudo-cider companies, and I took note that the label on the fizzing pump may bear little relation to the origin of the contents. Instead, we settled for a pint of perfectly acceptable Butcombe ale and awaited our second taxi of the day in the shelter of the extensive outdoor seating area while the traffic continued to howl past.

And so to Macawber House on the edge of Wincanton for our second night in the Far East. This delightful, highly individual B & B deserves a chapter to itself but suffice to say we were treated to a warm welcome, elegant rooms and a delicious supper before seeking out some cider in a nearby pub recommended earlier by our obliging taxi driver. A hearty dose of Cheddar Valley set us up for a good night's sleep while Roxie gratefully stretched out on a quilt kindly provided by our benevolent hostess.

After a fine, restorative breakfast we stepped out into a gentle, pale morning and strolled through the pleasant streets of Wincanton to the bus-stop in the municipal car park. The busy bus took us by a devious route back to Yeovil, where we switched buses for the familiar roll across the Somerset flatlands back to Taunton and the end of another brilliant border bash.

Wincanton to Frome

With Geoff

A blustery spring morning saw us delivered by Ginny to Penselwood Lane about three miles east of Wincanton and right on the border with Dorset. Accompanied by ranks of daffodils and primroses we followed the lane along the border to the northeast, serenaded by sprinklings of seasonal birdsong. We were atop a south-facing ridge, and occasional gaps in the bank revealed sweeping views across Dorset, maybe to the coast on a clearer day. Underfoot the squelchy, black mud made single file the best option, but the absence of Roxie's usual lead, temporarily misplaced and substituted with a shorter version, meant that I was continually hopping about to avoid shunting her rear end. Ever eager at this time of day she pressed on apace, regardless of my undignified discomfort. This is unknown and potentially deer-harbouring country, so the risk of releasing her outweighed the benefit of an unencumbered gait.

We were walking the southern edge of an odd protrusion of our eastern border at the point of which the Dorset/Wiltshire boundary line runs away to the east. We left the well-worn track and the mud, and took a footpath northward across some small, sloping fields dotted with an assortment of cattle, including a Hereford bull who viewed us with studied indifference. Perhaps on account of his presence we veered inadvertently a little westward and found ourselves pathless and way-marker-free. The sight of a man with a dog in the near-distance suggested the right track, so we retraced our steps past the sullen bull and descended the hill to meet Coombe Street, which runs back to the village of Penselwood. (We noticed that the road signs offer Penselwood or Pen Selwood, seemingly at random.) Checking out the history of the area I rather regret that our route missed out this village, which has been a lively spot in its time, with its fair share of the customary Somerset violence. (I can only wonder if an excess of cider on the previous evening may have interfered with my route planning such as to neglect this interesting little peninsula of Somerset.) As early as 658 the Saxons finally saw off the hapless Britons here, and in 1016 Edmund Ironside repelled the Danes led by Cnut The Great, though clearly not so great on this occasion. Alas, following the disaster of 1066, Britnod, the last Saxon incumbent of the manor, was displaced by yet another wicked Norman, one Roger Arundel.

We rejoined the border to begin the long northward trek along the ridge through the woods, here dominated by huge Scots pines. Once upon a time this whole area would have been native oak and ash forest, but these have long since fallen to the merciless axe, leaving a strip of mostly managed woodland following the border. I suppose we should be thankful and be grateful that not everything has been reduced to bleak arable prairies. There was little variation in the woodland scenery until we skirted Pen Hill, where the Somerset side is clad with a relatively recent plantation of beech, and with an old marksman's seat in a tree to the side of the path suggesting that deer may have been a problem in the plantation's younger days.

Our path joined the Macmillan Way as it follows the border northwards on the Somerset side. As usual the way-markers were less than comprehensive among the ephemeral forestry tracks, causing us to deviate a little around the western edge of the wood.

This inadvertent detour afforded us huge views to the west across the length of Somerset, with what can only be Exmoor in the far, hazy distance. Our 'alternative' footpath led us through the remains of a farmyard which made the word 'ramshackle' seem inadequate. The array of decomposing machinery was at least the equal of anything we have seen before, while the huge, rickety barns were in a class of their own, ranging from partial disintegration to total collapse. What dire circumstances could have brought about this sorry state? The liberal scattering of corrugated sheeting strewn around suggested that this is no place to be in a high wind.

We turned east onto the road for a short distance before rejoining the Macmillan Way northward, once more following the contour through deep woods parallel to the border. The steep hillside rising to the east hides Alfred's Tower from view which, I feel, is no great loss. This typically ostentatious, late 18th century folly was conceived to celebrate the end of the Seven Years war and the accession of George III and, more importantly, marks the place at which Alfred rallied his Saxons in 878 before sorting out the Danes once and for all. I wonder how England's noblest king would view such a monument to his mad, Hanoverian successor. (It is, perhaps, ironic, that a 'plane which crashed into the 40m tower in 1944 causing severe damage was a Noorduyn Norseman. The revenge of the Danes?)

Still in the woods we met our first human of the day: a lady with two terriers on leads. As she approached, the rough-coated brown one with a squashed face (Norfolk? Border?) appeared to go berserk, straining in our direction and yapping horribly. The ever-ready Roxie, thankfully also leashed, responded with a lunge and a meaningful look, and as the woman hurried away she admonished the still yapping terrier with, "Don't be so stupid. It would eat you." Correct.

The hillside above us was a more or less continuous pheasant pen, heavily fenced to protect the thousands of hapless poults which will be incarcerated here later in the year. As a life-long countryman I feel I have the right to object to these ghastly pheasant factories, most of which seem to cater for corporate junkets for comically-clad city types. The squirrel traps we were finding chained to trees at intervals along the trail are no more pleasing to me than the pheasant pens. The sturdy wooden boxes with convenient entrance holes at either end conceal heavy-duty snapper traps which, to my mind, are hardly more humane than the infamous and illegal gin traps. This is King's Warren Wood, the name indicating that rabbits rather than pheasants were the targets here in former times, and as we neared the end we came across a spring which is marked by an arched, stone structure with a couple of steps leading down to the water. Another heavy stone lying alongside bears the date 1841, but the purpose of this odd little edifice was not apparent. Roxie failed in her attempt to gain access to the water at the bottom of the steps, but the arch provided a convenient seat for a belated lunch so she settled for a share of the sandwiches and a drink from the water bottle.

We left the wood through a clearing onto the road where my sense of direction deserted me completely and I led us off to the west along a quiet road in the opposite direction from our required eastward route. I can only blame the lack of cider, the obscured sun and some extremely cavalier map-reading for this error, which was promptly revealed by the unexpected absence of woodland. Retracing our steps, we turned off the road into West End Wood, again following the Macmillan Way northwards in close parallel to the border. This is handsome, mature mixed woodland which continues into Trout Pond Wood where the scene changes: the tree mixture becomes dominated by towering conifers - probably Douglas Fir, but the foliage is too high to be sure - and the ground becomes boggy with a dense ground cover of Stinking Iris. A mile or two more of uneventful woodland brought us onto the road at Gare Hill, little more than a few cottages, a substantial church and a telephone box. Who the patrons of either of the latter are or were is something of a mystery, as this place is miles from anywhere.

A short step along a bit of tarmac and we re-entered the boggy woods heading north east along the border, with one foot in Somerset and the other in Wiltshire. The track along here is prettily named as Honey Pot Lane which, as it turns out, is rather less than appropriate. As we approached the Frome Road the sides of the path were polluted with junk of all sorts: bits of bicycles, electrical appliances, baby buggies and an assortment of domestic garbage littered the undergrowth. It is hard to imagine why the barbarians responsible for this were unable to find their way to a council tip or, should I say, recycling facility. And it got worse: where the track meets the road, a broad clearing was littered with rubbish, both domestic and commercial, in hideous quantity, and we could only wonder if its position right on the border means that neither Council is prepared to take responsibility.

The afternoon was wearing on and, to be honest, we had had about enough of the woods for today. Before summoning our taxi, we decided to cross the border to the village of Horningsham in the hope that the pub marked on the map might be both present and open. We were in luck and were welcomed into the Bath Arms by a genial young Rumanian barman who, unbidden, produced a welcome bowl of water for Roxie. She accepted the favour graciously then adopted her customary post-walk position, flat out on the bar floor, while we lamented the lack of decent cider while readily accepting a pint of Golden Apostle. Not Somerset, but good ale just the same.

We called our taxi, rather reluctantly, and finished our drinks. When I had phoned the proprietor of Arrow Taxis a couple of days before, I first enquired as to his willingness to transport a dog. (Some taxi people seem to be a bit precious about that sort of thing.) After a brief pause he asked what sort of dog and, when told she is a deerhound lurcher, he replied cheerfully that, "That'll be all right then." Given that she is both large and hairy, it's hard to imagine what sort of beast would be unacceptable to this accommodating chap. When I made this provisional booking, I was unable to tell him exactly where or when the pick-up would be, to which he replied that "That'll be all right then", and that he would book us in.

With Roxie draped across my lap in the back seat, our taxi hero ferried us back across the border to Frome station. My old granny used to say that 'things' go in threes, and on this trip the old adage certainly applied when it came to organisational pigs' ears: first the unorthodox route round Penselwood, then the wrong direction at West End Wood and, finally, a misreading of the train timetable such as to give us a three-quarters of an hour wait which we could have spent comfortably in the Bath Arms. Geoff was stoically tolerant, as ever, even though Frome station, it must be said, is a pretty grim place, and was deserted except for a pair of entangled teenagers.

To fill the time, we took a stroll around Frome's southern edge where the river is bordered by open fields somewhat reminiscent of Taunton's pleasant Longrun Meadow. We made our way in haste back to the station for Roxie's first-ever train ride, which she undertook with her usual equanimity, sprawling full-length on the carriage floor causing as much obstruction as possible, smiling at small children and unaccountably terrifying a lady in a headscarf, who appeared to be preparing to climb out of the window. A change of trains at Castle Cary, a pretty little town I seem to remember but a rather bleak railway outpost, saw us nicely on our way back to Taunton.

This long walk through the woods was hardly the most exciting of our border jaunts: woods are all very nice and peaceful and all that, but a whole day without a village, a pub (except as a finale) or any trace of cider makes for a long haul relieved, it should be noted, by some breathtaking views. The fact that we had been bordering both Longleat[1] and Stourhead estates may account for the absence of population, the whole area seemingly dominated by huge farms and extensive 'private' woodlands with little in between. Nevertheless, with thanks to Geoff for his continuing gracious forbearance, we looked forward to the next sortie into the north east corner of this endlessly varied county.

[1]I think it worth a mention that I had attempted to obtain permission to traverse a part of the Longleat Estate (not the bit with the lions) to follow the border but, as is so often the case these days, received no reply. I feel sure that the previous incumbent - he of the numerous 'wifelets' and supposedly lewd murals - would have viewed my request more favourably.

Interlude 6

Trespassing

I was just walking across a stubble field with the dog one winter morning when a tractor stopped by the gate and the bloke started waving his arms about. I waved back, of course, but he seemed to be a bit irate so I went over to see what was up.

I ought to say that I hadn't lived round here for long at that time. In the last 35 years or so I've been in three or four places within a 5-mile radius, but not right here, so I didn't know this bloke and he didn't know me. Anyway, I strolled over and said how d'you do.

"D'you know you're trespassing," he barked, in a not-very-friendly manner.

"Well, I suppose I am," I replied, as pleasantly as I could manage. "You got a problem with that?"

"Yes," he said, "I have. How d'you like somebody walking their dog in *your* garden?" (This is a classic outraged-farmer line.)

I looked over my shoulder at the 60-acre stubble field. "If my garden was that big I don't think I'd give a bugger," I said, with a cheerful smile.

He didn't seem very pleased. "I grow food crops in there," he shouted over the rumble of the tractor. "I don't want dogs crappin' all over it."

"Come off it," I shouted back. "Even if my dog was crappin' in your field, which he wasn't, a bit of dog crap's not a patch on the poisonous crap you spray all over it. Anyway, I daresay you might be ploughing it before you plant any more 'food crops', so I still can't see your problem. He was going a bit red and trying to interrupt, but I didn't give him the chance.

"Anyway," I went on, "what d'you do about all the badgers and foxes that crap in the stubble? Do you go shouting at them and all?"

He was a bit stuck there, so he went on to the next 'get off my land' standard. "Why don't you keep to the footpaths?" he yelled.

"Funny you should say that," I yelled back, "because I can see two from here that are what you might call 'obstructed'. One of them's ploughed up and the other's a foot deep in muck. What about a bit of give and take, then?"

He'd had about enough. "You're effin' trespassing." he roared, "and if I see you on my land again there'll be trouble."

"Hey, steady on," I roared back. "That's no way to talk to your employer.

"What!" I thought he was going to get down and have a go, but he saw the dog hackling up and thought better of it. "What d'you mean by that?"

"If it wasn't for *my* taxes paying for *your* subsidies, mate, you'd be on a bicycle not a bloody great tractor, so let's be a bit civil shall we."

He gave me and the dog the sort of look that would curdle milk. "I've told you. Keep off my land." And he revved up the tractor and zoomed off.

The next day there was a big, hand-painted notice on the field gate: "Private. Keep Out." Miserable bugger.

While I've got some sympathy for land-owners who genuinely suffer from vandalism and so on, the whole 'my land' thing is a funny old do, isn't it? It would be interesting to trace back the history of that stubble field, and thousands of others like it. It would be nice to know just who stole it, and when. It's a fair bet that it was William the bloody Conqueror, or one of his chums. Then came the Enclosures, from the 16th century onwards, and the job was done. Today it's reckoned that 0.6% of the population owns 50% of the land which, somehow, doesn't seem to be quite decent. The cruellest cut of all must be that large tracts of Somerset are owned by the Duchy of bloody *Cornwall*! No further comment.

Interesting to note that the title deeds of my little patch show that the mineral rights hereto belong to the *Bishop of Winchester*! This, along with the land itself, was probably gifted by good old Bill the Conq back in the 11th century. Hmmmm.

Seems to me that most land owners' ancestors might have been royal arse-lickers, thieves or murderers once upon a time. Makes you think.

Up North

Frome to Rudge

With Miranda

The Far East of Somerset is a hell of a way from Taunton - it took over an hour to drive to Frome. Public transport is tricky, to say the least so, to begin the long haul up the easternmost reaches of the County, we had to settle for another walk-and-drive session today.

On a beautiful spring morning we could find nowhere to park at the intended starting point of Lane End on the border south-east of Frome, so we drove a short hop over the border and back to begin at Lye's Green. Leaving the car on a convenient verge we set off northward through lush, rolling grassland dotted with large, prosperous farms, each with its smart, expensive name-plate on the gate. Groups of sleek beef cattle grazed with smug contentment and, whilst I rather resented their supercilious look, it was good to see some livestock outdoors after the empty plains of the south. The variety of agricultural practices in this varied county is broad to say the least, ranging from sheep grazing on the high moors to the summering cattle on the Levels, and from the arable prairies to the few remaining mixed holdings tucked into the valleys. With the possible exception of those prairies, each has its place in these chequered landscapes, and we can only hope that they are never totally homogenised by the brutal commercialisation of modern times.

As we left the lane and started into the fields on a dubiously-marked footpath we passed what must be the only ramshackle building in the area: a collection of tatty sheds and an unkempt paddock harbouring some very vocal but unseen dogs. No further way-markers were visible so we continued northwards across the fields, just on the Wiltshire side of the border, to Corsley Mill. Here a stile suggested that the path crosses an isolated garden, but the inhabitant assured us that the path was blocked by building works, and offered us an alternative route up the hill, condemning us to further unmarked wanderings. Half way up Roxie snapped into Full Alert and, sure enough, a roebuck broke cover and made off through a scrubby bit of woodland, its white, powder-puff tail flashing. The thwarted hound gave us her usual resentful look, deprived again of the joy of the chase.

With sweeping views to the west, south and east we found a convenient if unofficial track and climbed towards the A3098, still just on the Wilts side. To the south we could make out the sharp, unmistakable shape of Cley Hill (239m) a couple of miles away. This megalithic hill fort has, more recently, been a favourite spot for UFO-watchers as well as a notable chalkland SSSI, but it's in Wiltshire, so no more of that. At the top of the hill we made our way along a meander of footpaths through a collection of over-grazed pony paddocks complete with ratty buildings and makeshift fences, watched by a trio of disdainful alpacas. One day I really must get someone to explain why they keep these supercilious South Americans instead of proper sheep. We hit the main road, fortunately blessed with a pavement, on the western edge of the village of Chapmanslade, still just in Wiltshire, and headed for the pub and lunch.

After a pleasant interlude in the pub garden, where Roxie was subjected to almost obsequious attention from a woman admirer, we began the return trip, this time well and truly on the Somerset side. The paths are well signed (well done, Mendip District Council) and took us steadily downhill to the meandering Rodden Brook. A group of Badger-faced sheep (a rare breed indeed) watched us circumspectly as we crossed a couple of wooden bridges over the brook, overlooked by yet another impressive Georgian house. We climbed out of the shallow valley through more beautifully-kept grassland with more well-fed beef cattle lazily watching our progress. Almost all the farm-houses round here look like Georgian mansions with all the trimmings, and words like 'recession' and 'rural poverty' seem like a foreign language. It would be interesting if not horrifying to know the sources of the money which supports the obvious affluence of this part of Somerset.

Before rejoining the road at Lane End, the point from which we intended to start this morning, we passed the charmingly-named Tits Wood. Whether this refers to the birds of the genus Paridae or to the nature of its ownership we are unable to say.

A short step along the busy main road gained access to a barely-noticeable footpath running up hill across a couple of fields which, we were confident, would bring us back to the car. Our confidence was well founded so, flushed with navigational triumph, we collapsed on the verge to enjoy a well-earned drink - only tea, alas. Someone has to drive.

North of the A3098 there is a dire shortage of footpaths anywhere near the border, so we opted to drive this section on minor roads less than a mile to the west of The Line to the conjoined villages of Rudge and Lower Rudge. All the buildings here, without exception, are impossibly lovely, built from the glowing local limestone and, again, the affluence of this part of the County is glaringly apparent. I hesitate to say it, but the feel of the place is uncomfortably reminiscent of the Cotswolds! It is interesting to note that the rather stern Methodist chapel (built in 1839) is the only public building in these villages.   It would be even more interesting to know the demographic of this, and the other lovely villages in this area and to see how many 'locals' are resident here.

Somewhat overawed, we left Rudge and headed for home over more sweeping acres of grass towards Beckington, where the next leg of the border stroll will begin.

Beckington to Farleigh Hungerford

With Lorna

Another glorious spring morning found us in golden-stone Beckington, about one and a half miles west of the border. Although only about 100m above sea level, this whole rolling, grassy country dotted with patches of deep green woodland gives the impression of a high plateau and, again, the presence of opulence is unmistakeable.

At mid-morning there was little sign of life in this picture-book village as we left it via the lush green of the cricket ground next to the impressive, modern village hall. Our route follows the Macmillan Way leading northwards but here, blatantly contradicting the map, the path deviated around the glaring yellow of a vast field of oil-seed rape. This must be a good year for subsidies on this insidious 'yellow peril' which, to me, looks hideously unnatural, smells overpowering, and is of dubious benefit to the environment despite the delight of commercial bee-keepers. They should be mindful of the fact that the spray regime on rape is a threat to all insects, beneficial or otherwise. (The honey yield from this ever-increasing crop is exceptionally high, but the honey itself is miserably bland and requires to be removed from the hive within a fortnight of its gathering or the wretched stuff will set like concrete and be of no use to man or bee. Small-scale bee-keepers, such as I was, detest it.)

Contrary to the map the unmarked diversion led us along the edge of the mega-field in parallel with the roaring A36. At the corner of the field, the path, what there was of it, faded out completely, but we spotted a dog-walker and sought guidance. While his chirpy, short-coat collie chatted up the flirtatious Roxie he pointed us to a well-camouflaged path leading out to the main road. This would be a hazardous crossing at the best of times, but a quick dash took us across unscathed and we rejoined the Macmillan Way on a tarmac lane leading to the village of Rode. This is another delightful postcard village where all the buildings, with no apparent exceptions, are lovely, including the sturdy Methodist Primary School. (In a county where Church of England schools predominate this is unusual and must reflect the campaigns of John Wesley among the north Somerset miners in the 18th century, though the old mining areas are some distance from here to the north and west.) The obvious prosperity of Rode and of the other pretty villages in the area was derived mostly from wool originally, the trade thriving from the 16th to the early 19th centuries. At one time at least five mills graced the convenient meanders of the River Frome, allowing the accumulation of wealth sufficient to fund the building of numerous 'great' houses in the vicinity. From the look of the cottages even the peasantry did reasonably well out of the proceeds, though I feel sure they and their descendants have long gone.

We were a little early in the day to try the cider-compliance of the very picturesque pub so we pressed on through the village, Roxie pacing along elegantly until distracted by a couple of cats which, wisely, beat a rapid retreat. Other than the felines there was little sign of life, supporting the view that this once-bustling market village, even known as a 'town' at one time, is now another sad dormitory for Bath and Bristol. The ranks of gleaming, outsize cars lining, and spoiling, the streets suggested that this may also be a haven for incoming retirement refugees.

A short stretch of the Macmillan Way along a private road took us back to the border where it joins and follows the Frome northwards. The path, just on the Wiltshire side, passes through steep woodland overlooking the river, the understory prettily dotted with Violets and Wood Anemones in profusion and with the spear-head leaves of Wild Garlic promising delights to come. Below, the course of the river is broken by weirs and channels which once must have been the trappings of the old mills, and while we looked down on the tranquillity of sliding water we were surprised by a pair of Goosanders flying downstream. These spectacular diving ducks, which we last saw on the rushing Barle, are more associated with the rapids of Exmoor than with the gently-flowing Frome, but here they are, the drake unmistakeable in his bottle-green, black and white livery.

Coming out of the wood the path descends to the river bank across a lush meadow, and we took a break sitting on the bank watching the scores of tiny fish in the shallows. This lovely stretch, reminiscent of Wind in the Willows, is a half-size version of the placid Avon running through our childhood village, now purloined by the so-called North Somerset. Hurrumph! We waited awhile, hoping for a sight of a Kingfisher but, despite the teeming fry, the jewel of the river failed to put in an appearance.

Reluctantly leaving this idyllic spot we crossed back into Somerset over a beautiful little three-span foot bridge leading to the hamlet of Tellisford, noting as we passed a small flotilla of large fish, probably trout by the look of them, cruising in the shallow water below. As we admired the fish, a rough-coated, brown terrier joined us on the bridge. Bearing in mind our last raucous encounter with such a creature in West End Wood, I anticipated some action, which would be a little uncomfortable in the confines of the narrow bridge. This one, though, was of a friendly disposition and exchanged cordial sniffs and greetings with Roxie while we chatted with its elegant lady companion.

The imposing and somehow fitting Tellisford Mill sits squarely on the river bank on the Somerset side. This ancient Saxon structure, mentioned in the Domesday Book, has been significantly updated, and a notice board affixed to the wall informed us that it has been equipped with a two-ton bronze-alloy turbine which actually generates real electricity for the local area. This brilliant enterprise is a classic example of what can be done for local energy production while in no way spoiling the beauty of this charming spot.

A steep flight of steps, our first real climb of the day, took us out of the valley and through the cluster of immaculate cottages which mark the edge of Tellisford. Keeping to the Macmillan Way, with the border and the river a couple of hundred yards to the east, we approached the magnificence of Manor Farm. The iron railings lining the drive are painted a fetching cream, and the gateposts are topped with green-painted pineapples. Yes, pineapples. This is a return to Georgian opulence if ever there was. Even the handsome sheep, complete with a brace of lambs apiece, appeared to be looking down their noses at us.

Rounding the huge, elegant farmhouse, if such it still is, we took to the fields and encountered, yet again, a paucity of way-markers. A number of hedges appeared to have been grubbed out in the name of efficiency, so we hazarded a guess and headed off across the arable wasteland, the saving grace being a flock of seventy linnets twittering and skittering over the stubble. A recently-planted woodland and scattered pheasant feeders and rearing pens indicated the main enterprise hereabouts, but more of that later. Somewhat confused by some slight disparities with the map, we stopped for a lunch break in a shady corner of a field, where I checked our position on my recently-acquired electronic location finder: a ten-figure map reference, no less! Having established exactly where we were, only a little off course, we could enjoy the magnificent views across the river valley to the east into Wiltshire. With lunch completed we roused the dozing Longdog and headed down the hill to rejoin our appointed path.

Descending through a small patch of mixed woodland we came across an old cable-drum carrying a considerable length of baler twine festooned with scores of strips of multi-coloured plastic which seem to have been painstakingly cut from old feed bags. Presumably, when extended off the drum, this cunning device will present a fluttering barrier along the nearby drove to deflect the pheasants trying to escape the deadly combination of beaters, dogs and flying lead. I have no objection to the occasional pheasant for the pot, far from it, but this commercial pheasant farming really is a nasty business.

We rejoined our path at the bottom of the wood and made our exit across a grassy, sheep-strewn field sloping down to the river and the border, the path joining a quiet tarmac lane leading northward for the last leg of today's jaunt towards Farleigh Hungerford. A steepish climb brought us to a cluster of cottages and a strange, stone-built, cylindrical water tower about twenty feet high and ten feet across. A nearby notice informed us that it formerly supplied water to the Farleigh Hungerford Estate and the hamlet of Tellisford, before becoming 'redundant' in the 1970's. Almost opposite stands the church of St Leonard, a modestly handsome edifice which was 'remodelled' in 1856. It was probably in need by then, as it was first consecrated in 1443. It contains some interesting artefacts from various stages in its long history but it was, alas, locked, so we had to make do with admiring some of the stained glass from the outside.

As we headed up the hill toward the A366 we spotted an enormous Gothic Revival pile over to our left. We took this to be the famous Farleigh Castle, but the manicured rugby pitches between the road and the edifice should have provided a clue: this is, in fact, Farleigh House (some house), now the administrative home of Bath Rugby! The house was built in the late 18th and early 19th centuries, mostly using stone from the by-then ruined castle. It has since passed through a selection of well-manicured hands, including an optical company and the actor Oliver Reed's brother, before being acquired by a kindly benefactor for the use of the rugby club. At least their offices and training grounds are still in Somerset even though their real home, the hallowed Rec., has been netted by the upstart BANES.

Having made pretty good progress today we decided (or, rather, Lorna decided) that we deserved a cultural visit to the real Farleigh Castle, which is just down the road. (I must point out that the paucity of cultural visits so far has been down to geography rather than to my plebeian inclination. Well, that's my story.) To say that this castle has a chequered history fails to do its turbulent past any justice. Built in the late 14th century, probably on the site of a stolen Saxon manor, it was the home of the Hungerford dynasty for over 300 years. This lot were even more tricksy and peculiar than most other land-owning families of the time, changing allegiance in the War of the Roses and the Civil War such that, one way and another, they managed to retain possession of their lands and a more or less undamaged castle. One of them rode with Henry V at Agincourt while another was executed with Thomas Cromwell in 1540, possibly for homosexuality. Their reign finally came to an end in 1686 with Edward the Spendthrift, who was forced to sell off the castle to pay his debts. What a crew. Subsequently the castle fell into disrepair and was plundered for building materials before some restoration was attempted in the 20th century. It is currently in the hands of English Heritage, and is well worth a visit, with some impressive towers still standing, a delightful, ancient chapel and a well-preserved priest's house. Roxie was taking full advantage of the cool flagstones of the latter before we were tactfully evicted by a young attendant - dogs are allowed in the grounds, we were told, but not in the buildings. We wondered which of the crabby-looking visitors 'snitched' on us.

After placating the deeply-offended Roxie with an ice cream we wandered down to the car park where, we were told, a footpath leads to the back door of the Hungerford Arms and, sure enough, a steep climb out of the valley through a pretty wood led us to our objective. We were rewarded with magnificent views over the valley to the north and east from the pub garden, while the affable landlord pointed out the several millionaires' residences dotted around between the patches of woodland. All these are 'tastefully restored' buildings of great antiquity and beauty. The excellent pint of Black Rat cider hailed from Melksham (in Wiltshire!) but was still excellent for all that.

We summoned our taxi from the same worthy outfit which transported us to Frome a few weeks ago. The cheerful young driver seemed delighted with Roxie who, slightly disconcertingly, stood on the back seat and licked his neck as we drove back to Beckington. He deposited us safely at our car and bestowed God's blessings upon us before departing with a merry wave. As we headed back west into the sunset we reflected on yet another delightful day in what our pious taxi driver would surely consider to be God's own county.

Norton St Philip to Foxcote

With Lorna

Even on a pale, overcast morning the mellow Bathstone cottages of
Norton St Philip glowed behind a profusion of Wisteria blossom.
The village is soaked in history, claiming the oldest pub in England
(the George, first licensed in 1397), visited by Samuel Pepys in 1668
and being closely linked with Somerset's darkest days in 1685.
Monmouth garrisoned here and fought a "small" battle on the edge
of the village: the rebels won this skirmish with few losses while the
graphically-named Blood Hill recalls the greater casualties among
the King's men. Sadly, the success was short-lived, and the Duke's
visit was soon followed by that of the infamous Judge Jefferies, who
executed a dozen local men in unpleasant fashion as part of his
notorious Bloody Assizes.

We walked out of the village along Wellow Lane heading for the
border half a mile or so to the north. On a garage door we spotted a
notice proclaiming a more recent rebellion: "The Pitchfork Rebels
(.org). Norton St Fullup. Excessive Housing Rebellion 2013-14."
This presumably refers to the ghastly new housing 'development'
which assaults the eye just as you enter this otherwise lovely village
from the south, and it seems that the common pattern of crazy
planning permission has been repeated here. It would appear that

the protesters were on a loser once again, though it would be interesting to know the provenance of these latter-day rebels.

As we passed a beautifully restored old mill, a territorial cairn terrier followed us along the fence with a deal of agitated yapping which totally failed to disturb the loping indifference of a preoccupied Roxie. The cheery human occupant of the garden assured us the terrier was only "saying hello", and we noted, once again and without surprise, the accents of the East in this remarkably affluent territory.

The steep-sided valley contains small fields interspersed with woodland, the whole picture, complete with a few grazing beef cattle, being reminiscent of our childhood not so far away along the Avon near Bath. The dense, seemingly unmanaged patches of woodland were carpeted with Ramsons, their white flowers sparkling like stars under the canopy, but the temperature was still a little low for them to release their characteristic garlic odour. On a warm day this valley bottom must smell like a French kitchen.

We crossed the border into the spurious BANES, then turned off the road to the west over a footbridge, with a ford as an option, and climbed a steep track along the edge of a dense mixed wood. With steep valleys to the north and south we left the wood behind and mounted the top of a broad ridge. Although the actual altitude is only about 138m, we seemed to be on top of the world, with glorious views over this valley-fissured country to left and right. Up here, the land is flatter and gently rolling so, predictably, many hedges have been grubbed out and the arable prairies prevail.

At Upper Baggridge Farm now, apparently, a collection of 'tasteful conversions', we joined the tarmac lane which would take us southward and back to the border. While the fields are huge and were daubed with the glaring yellow of oil-seed rape, the roadside banks offered a more subtle palette of botanical diversity, with clouds of Cow Parsley, Red Campion, Vetch and Violets. At Knoll

Farm (more of that later) we re-crossed the border into 'official' Somerset and began the return journey to Norton St Philip to retrieve the car.

Where the lane joins the A366, the map showed a pub symbol at the crossing designated as Tucker's Grave Bottom, which surely warranted investigation. Sure enough, the pub squats on the corner, with what looks like a farmyard as a car park to the rear and a drab frontage right on the main road. A stern sign on the closed, paint-peeling front door miserably stated "No Dogs", which is never a good omen, and there was little sign of life within. Skirting round to the back again we found a small courtyard garden with a few deserted tables, but I deemed it too chilly to sit outside in the shade and, besides, there was no olfactory evidence of lunch on the go. We opted out and headed for the fields, thankful that we'd brought a packed lunch, just in case.

(In fairness, I am bound to add that I have since checked out Tucker's Grave on the interweb and found some reviews describing a fine, traditional cider house unchanged for 200 years. The reviews have the feel of having been written by London visitors, who wouldn't know a traditional pub with decent cider if it fell on their silver 4x4's but, even so, I might be tempted to a revisit if it weren't for that not-very-traditional "No Dogs" sign.)

We stopped for a brief lunch break on the bank of a tiny stream with a background soundtrack of tractors cultivating the fields on the far side, then we continued on the path which follows the stream back to Norton St Philip. The stream soon swelled into a small and very pretty river running through a narrow, steep-sided valley where we were stopped in our tracks by great swathes of swaying Cowslips adorning the uncut little fields on our side of the water. I have not seen such a profusion of this lovely, homely flower in its natural habitat for fifty years or more, and the delight and nostalgia almost brought me to tears. To complete the picture, the opposite bank was clothed with a blanket of Primroses under the coppiced Hazel. Roxie was unimpressed by the flora but suddenly took a keen interest in a large hole at the top of the bank. This was not substantial enough for a badger sett and was too big and clearly more noseworthy than a rabbit burrow so, on hands and knees, I applied my own pitifully inferior nose to the hole and detected the unmistakeable whiff of fox. We led her away under protest, as I tried to explain to her that persecuting foxes is both unpleasant and unnecessary. The bridge over the river is guarded at both ends by awkward stiles which caused the rangy hound some inconvenience as the bottom bar was too low for her to wriggle under. Instead, she contrived to scrabble over the top in a thoroughly awkward manner, seemingly oblivious to the fact that she is capable of clearing such obstacles in an easy bound. Perhaps she believed the rough plank steps were obligatory?

Collecting the car from our starting point at Norton St Philip we drove the short distance west along the A366 to Faulkland. This is one of those unfortunate villages strung out along and bisected by a main road and, like most of them, appears to be lacking in charm. It also lacks the focal point of a church, being blessed with only a rather stern chapel and even the pub fails to look particularly inviting. We left the car by the roadside for lack of any other parking and took a bridleway northward back towards the border. It was heartening to find an extensive and well-used badger sett system alongside the path right on the edge of the village, showing no sign of interference or persecution. Clearly, they are well away from the wretched cull zone here.

The grassy bridleway returned us to the border at Knoll Farm where, earlier, we had turned back eastwards to collect the car. It bears a less-than-friendly 'Our Dogs Bite' sign on the gate but, fortunately for them, they were not around to test Roxie's mettle. Venturing over the border into BANES yet again, we followed a deeply-rutted track through a handsome mixed wood, passing a wooden building which announced itself as the HQ of the Knoll Shoot: another commercial pheasantry, no doubt. The ruts in the rocky, yellow clay were so deep as to make walking down the steep slope a tricky operation, and it's a wonder that vehicles can negotiate it at all.

Emerging from the wood onto Faulkland Lane, a very slightly-flagging Lorna made the brave decision to turn north and follow another stretch of border towards the hamlet of Stony Littleton rather than take the easy route south and straight back to Faulkland. At Dairy Cottage we took a footpath westward parallel to Wellow Brook, passing almost through the garden and facing the implacable gaze of a trio of alpacas and a couple of donkeys. (What is it about donkeys that makes them so appealing? Is it those disproportionate ears or the serene expression that makes you want to befriend them? Alpacas, on the other hand, are unlovely beasts, and certainly never carried Jesus anywhere.)

From this point the way-markers were absent, and we found ourselves adrift in a vast field of emerging tick-beans where a glorious chestnut hare, the size of a small dog, bounded away along the contour, fortunately below Roxie's sight-line. We escaped from the bean field by negotiating a gap in the barbed-wire fence and sliding down a steep bank to the floor of the lovely little valley cradling the Wellow Brook. Cuckoo Flowers (aka Ladies' Smock) lined the banks of this delightful meandering little river overhung with spring-green trees. The high banks and clear, shallow water seemed ideal for trout, but there was no sign of life, and the blankets of rippling weed and cool stillness lent an oddly mysterious air to this magical place.

The valley broadens out as the path meets a neat stone bridge carrying a rough old road over the river. Next to the ancient bridge, on the near river bank, stand seven large, flat-topped concrete pyramids whose function defied our imaginations. They are far from picturesque; in fact, they are little short of ugly but, we agreed, their intimidating bulk would make their removal a serious and expensive undertaking. We climbed the steep, gravelly road out of the valley in the direction of the hamlet of Foxcote, crossing back into

Somerset and puffing a little as we reached the top of the hill. We turned off into a bridleway named as Tenantsfield Lane which follows this convoluted bit of border southwards to take us back to Faulkland. On high ground again, we looked down to the east over another beautiful little valley with the border running along the bottom. Once again, if God has his own country this is probably it. This broad lane must once have been a significant thoroughfare between Faulkland and the cluster of hamlets we have left behind but it showed little sign of use other than by the boot-marks of walkers now, and rather few of those by the look of it. This is all the more odd as there were plenty of horses around: in an adjacent field a bunch of around thirty assorted equines, most with at least some cob in them, were grazing peacefully, and we were bound to wonder who owns them and what they are for.   A little further on, a nominally-electrified enclosure almost retained a couple of Old Spot sows and a handful of piglets no more than three weeks old, the latter seeming to be unaware of the electrics, scampering in and out with piggy glee. The map shows no habitation in the vicinity so we wondered again who might be the custodian of these cheery porkies in their idyllic little piggery.

The path now descends into one more deep, grassy valley and crosses a boggy stream before we tackled the long, steady ascent over broad fields back to Faulkland. Looking back, we could oversee the pattern which had prevailed for most of the day: big, mostly arable fields on the flatter uplands, with much smaller, hedged and partly wooded pockets on the steeper valley sides. The bits of arable prairie notwithstanding, this is beautiful and comforting country, and it was a real delight to follow the border through it.

On the long drive back home, we stopped for refreshment at a welcoming pub on the edge of the Levels, where Roxie received adoration and dog-treats from the tiny daughter of the house. When finally left in peace she stretched out in her customary post-border-

walk pose and slept, while we enjoyed some good grub and just a
drop of cider.

Foxcote to Clapton and on to Harptree Hill

With Geoff

Reaching what used to be the southern fringe of Somerset's Industrial North would take half a day by public transport, so Geoff and I had agreed to meet just south of Radstock and to operate a two-car shuffle for this section of the border. From White Post we drove to Chilcompton, deposited one car at the church then drove back to Foxcote to begin the day's sortie.

Parking in this compact little valley-bottom settlement proved to be impossible, so we drove over the bridge and up the steep incline, crossing the border into the usurping BANES. A broad track afforded sufficient space to squeeze the car under a hedge, so we disembarked and set off westward along a tree-lined cycle path overlooking the picturesquely meandering Wellow Brook down below. When we reached Bridge 33 on the surprisingly wiggly course of the old Somerset and Dorset railway we realised that we had overshot the obscure south-bound footpath which purported to cross the brook and take us back to the border. Descending off the embankment through a wedge of woodland we wandered about in a patch of scrubby ground which is the site of an old colliery, and eventually found our way across the water and climbed out of the valley, heading south to the oddly-named Green Parlour. This turned out to be nothing more than an eponymous farm and a few cottages, where we turned west back over the border on a short stretch of lane leading to Writhlington.

Here we met a chaotic, traffic-light-ridden, road-works-mangled junction with the A362 which we managed to cross without loss, then followed the border on a sharp dog's leg around an enormous school looking more like a collection of huge warehouses. Among other distinctions, Writhlington School houses the largest collection of orchids outside Kew, a fact which strikes me as being remarkable, especially as the school is technically just outside Somerset. A footpath along the border soon turns southwards along the drive of Huish House, another impressive pile presumably built on the proceeds of coal mining and last sold in 2007 for £1.6 million! I was in the process of easing Roxie under a stile when the top bar detached itself, leaving me flat on my back with the timber wedged across my chest. Roxie looked back with what appeared to be disdain while Geoff readily accepted what he saw as an ideal photo-opportunity.

By-passing the grand house, we climbed an embankment to join a cycle path on the course of yet another disused railway line heading south. This took us a mile or so south of the border to the village of Kilmersdon, where a minor detour led to the Jolliffe Arms, a pleasant, dog-friendly establishment apparently still in the ownership of the Jolliffe Estate. This is another astonishing example of how William the Norman's henchmen have managed to hang on to their plunder for centuries, this Jolliffe lot beginning in what is now Tyne and Wear before somehow extending their holdings to include a significant chunk of Somerset. I digress. We had to settle for a pint of Thatchers Dry, as the young lady behind the bar explained that they used to serve the real stuff but "...it got 'em fightin', so we had to pack it in." Such a slur on the reputation of proper cider surprised and saddened me, especially as the only apple-based beverage rightfully earning an association with violence was a nasty, bottled, commercial concoction known as 'Natch', made from foreign concentrate by the erstwhile Taunton Cider Co. in Norton Fitzwarren. Good cider, on the other hand, surely has a mellowing, benevolence-inspiring effect?

Returning to the border we took on the steep Jack and Jill Hill, marked by a handsome relief carving in local stone. The hill is reputedly the site of the well-known nursery rhyme, and local lore has it that the surname Gilson, not uncommon hereabouts, derives from 'Jill's son', the illegitimate result of the dalliance on the hill. How Jack's cracked skull came about we can only guess. At the top of the hill we passed the bustling primary school with its eye-catching Jack and Jill mural on the wall, turned into Waterside Lane (no sign of any water) and descended across grassy fields along the border to the industrial outskirts of Radstock. The border turns sharply south as we reached the A367 so, to avoid the main road, we ventured again into BANES and strolled along a residential street leading to the Radstock Railway Centre. Had this still been in Somerset-proper we should have taken a look but, in haste to get back to the border, we took a well-used footpath through the wooded Silver Street Nature Reserve, then crossed a school playing field swarming with home-going kids and assorted dog-walkers. The pretty Riverside Walk runs alongside the River Somer, crossing back over the border in the direction of Chilcompton where we left the car this morning. This would have been the easy option, but we decided to press on over the fields to Clapton, which seemed to have the makings of a good starting point for tomorrow.

Sure enough, a few more sloping fields and stone-slab stiles took us to the Crown Inn, where we refreshed ourselves with a swift half of Thatchers and gained permission to leave the car in their car-park in the morning. A rather wistful lady in the bar expressed the wish that she could be walking with us, but her husband seemed less keen.

We waded back to Chilcompton through waist-deep grass, the long descent affording birds'-eye views of the south-western corner of Radstock tucked prettily into the folds of the edge of Mendip. We loaded up one weary dog and negotiated the road-works-ridden centre of Radstock to collect the second car from Foxcote, then drove back to the Fromeway Inn just on the 'wrong' side of the border on the edge of the town. The out-of-county location was more than compensated for by the warmth of the welcome from the genial landlord, the comfortable rooms and excellent dinner. The business, formerly a butchers' shop as well as an inn, has been in the family since 1852 with John, the present incumbent, taking over from his father in 1976 and only relinquishing the butchery in 2009.

After dinner we returned to the bar where Roxie stretched out on the floor in as obstructive a position as possible (as usual) and was stepped over and admired by a steady flow of fellow customers. "Christ, I thought it was a bloody 'orse," one remarked cheerfully. Over our last pint the landlord kindly pointed out where we could take a pre-breakfast dog-walk if required, and so we retired, with all well with the world once again.

At seven next morning, I looked out of the window over the surprisingly green and wooded valleys to the south, and we ventured out on the recommended early morning dog-walk. The well-worn paths across the fields were deserted except for one distant dog-walker but, in the circumstances, I felt obliged to employ an unfamiliar poo-bag and the corresponding depository. (I say unfamiliar not because we are scornful of such refinements but because, in our usual unpopulated haunts, Roxie is discreet in her defaecatory habits.)

After a fine breakfast we were off for another two-car manoeuvre, the first drop being in the car-park in East Harptree Woods, which would be our final destination for the day. Geoff was a little concerned about leaving his rather smart car here in the wilderness, but I assured him that on weekdays the local barbarians only steal 4x4's, pick-ups and tractors. We drove back to the Crown at Clapton, left my totally undesirable car in the car-park and set off northwards to rejoin the border and to follow it from the slag-heaps of Midsomer

Norton to the high plateau and sweeping views of the eastern Mendip Hills.

Roxie had, by now, acquired the hang of these stone-slab stiles and took them like a steeplechaser as we followed a stream through more deep grass liberally dotted with docks and nettles. I guess that the steep slopes and corresponding small fields contribute to what seems like the rather laissez-faire style of farming I associate with my youth in north Somerset and is certainly a contrast to the manicured prairies down south. At the side of the field we found a fenced-off area enclosing an extensive badger sett system, and we blessed the farmer in his absence. He is obviously not taken in by the nonsensical, science-free views of the Government/NFU condemning the badger as a scapegoat for the farming industry's inability/unwillingness to control bovine TB by appropriate husbandry practices.

With badgers and other nocturnal animals well out of the way at this time of day the liberated Roxie could run free, bounding over the long grass like a dolphin breaking the waves, and clearly enjoying the unfamiliar smells. Then it was back on the leash for a short stretch of tarmac taking us north to Langley Down Lane where we turned westward through a small wood along the top of a north-facing ridge. In the distance, presumably in the vicinity of Paulton, an unnaturally conical slag-heap, stern and grey, broods over what was once a coal-mining area rivalling South Wales. I suppose we should be grateful that this is the only visible reminder of the grim industrial past.

Roxie's nose was working overtime as she followed the numerous deer-slots in the thick Mendip clay along the path. It was another glorious morning, the wood full of birdsong (Blackcaps, Robins, Blackbirds) as we stepped through the spangling light dappled over the woodland floor.

Leaving the wood and turning north we descended from the ridge over cornfields and crossed the border just to the south of Farrington Gurney. Away from the main road this is a pretty village with much evidence of community activity, and it seems a pity that it is not only bisected but trisected, if that's a word, by two main roads. We crossed the A37 and followed Pit Lane along the border for a mile or so before turning off on a bridleway as it veers off to the south-west. On the map, Chewton Wood bears the little blue wader symbol signifying a nature reserve, and it is certainly wild enough, with mature oak and ash rising out of boggy ground-cover and with some dubious, little-used paths. Here, Roxie encountered her first single-plank bridge over a stream and sauntered across with delicate ease.

Emerging from the wood we found ourselves on a hard-surfaced track, meaning that the wayward woodland paths had taken us a little further south than anticipated, a couple of hundred yards south of the border. The track leads to a tarmac lane just east of the village of Litton so, as it was surely lunchtime or thereabouts, we stayed with the lane and headed for the pub through a picturesque collection of pretty cottages. For a start, the village-side entrance to the pub is forbidden to all but "disabled vehicles" (presumably vehicles for the disabled) so we circumnavigated around a busy B road to a huge, empty car-park. The wretched place was closed! On a Thursday lunchtime! The several elaborate signs proclaiming the likes of 'Genuine Pizza Oven' etc. were little consolation, especially as we came but lightly equipped with provisions. We concluded that this architecturally pleasant place must have become one of those ghastly 'gastro-pubs' which is now in the inevitable process of biting the dust. Leaving a rain-cloud of curses upon them, we took our lives in our hands along the B3114 to find a bridleway heading southwest in close parallel with the border.

The 'bridleway' turned out to be a steep climb up a narrow, rocky stream bed, and I would certainly hesitate to take a horse either up or down it while Geoff, on the other hand, enthused about its potential for mountain-biking, presumably downward. The joys of bicycling, mountain or otherwise, are beyond my comprehension. Each to his own, I suppose. The slippery path runs just inside a dense, boggy wood with signs of pheasant pens and feeders in the undergrowth, so there must be alternative access in there somewhere for the quads and 4x4's favoured by the 'keeping fraternity.

Reaching the summit, we descended a relatively gentle slope to meet a small road up hill and, where we rejoined the border at the top, were rewarded with truly breath-taking views to the north over the huge expanse of water which is Chew Valley lake glittering in the bright afternoon sun. The foreground was a delightful patchwork of fields and hamlets generously dotted with the darker greens of woodlands leading to the wide waters of the lake and the limestone hills around Bath in the background. It seems a crime that this lovely swathe of country is no longer recognised as part of true Somerset. Although the map shows numerous disused mine-shafts on the slopes around us it is hard to imagine that this bucolic scene was once scarred with mine workings.

A bridleway across a couple of well-grazed fields, complete with dozing Fresians, took us along the ridge to rejoin the road alongside East Harptree Wood where Geoff's car was parked, hopefully still intact. The afternoon seemed relatively young so, bravely or foolishly, we decided to carry on along the border on the Monarch's Way for a couple of miles then circle back to the car through the wood. (Was our decision coloured by the tantalizing little blue tankard symbol on the map, or had we learned our lesson by now?) We descended into Garrow Bottom and laboriously climbed the other side, perhaps beginning to regret this bravado-fuelled extension. Even Roxie was flagging in the heat (she is a sprinter by trade, after all) but she plodded on with commendable canine stoicism without complaint, even though she isn't quite tall enough to appreciate the continuing fabulous views to the north.

Joining the Old Bristol Road at last, half way up Harptree Hill, we were confronted by a truly woeful sight: The Wellsway Inn was not only closed but is "Available for Private Functions Only". What is wrong with the pubs in this part of the world? Two in one day! Disappointed but unbroken we retraced our steps back to East Harptree Woods and the carpark. Geoff's car stood unmolested, as promised, so we drove back to Clapton where a swift half and a bowl of water fortified us for the trip home. A pre-prepared pheasant casserole and some real cider provided a fitting end to what had been another tough but glorious jaunt along the border.

Interlude 7

Pubs

Sunday lunchtime. We walked into this very picturesque country pub on the edge of the Brendons, noting the 'No Muddy Boots' sign propped outside the door.

The landlord, who bore an unnerving resemblance to Peter O'Toole when past his prime, eyed us up.

"I hope those boots aren't muddy," he growled, in a pretty convincing O'Toole voice.

"Just washed them," I said. "They're fine."

"Well," he said, almost defensively, "you wouldn't want people walking across *your* carpets in muddy boots, would you?"

"No, I suppose not," I replied, with a cheery smile, "but I don't run a pub."

Stand-off. He looked us up and down again and, possibly swayed by my glamorous companion, grudgingly conceded. "Mmmm. What can I get you then?"

"Got any decent cider ?"

"Nothing you'd like," he grunted. "I've only got this bottled rubbish. And d'you want to know why?"

"I expect you're going to tell me."

"Yes, it's Lionel bloody Blair."

"I thought he was a song and dance man."

"Yep. And the bloody Prime Minister as well, more's the pity."

There followed a rant against our Beloved Leader of the time, with particular reference to his single-handed destruction of the rural economy, leading to the drastic reduction in cider consumption. This latter abomination means that the real stuff, which doesn't keep well, doesn't sell fast enough. Hence the 'bottled rubbish only' policy. No wonder he's such a grumpy sod.

Settling for a pint of excellent local bitter, we ordered what turned out to be a first-class Sunday lunch served, and presumably cooked, by the Grumpy Sod's charming and doubtless long-suffering wife.

Despite the slight lack of warmth in the welcome at this hostelry, the quality of the lunch was sufficient to draw me back when next walking in the area. (It was also the only pub for miles.) We arrived at 1.45, noticing this time the "Lunch Served 12.00 - 2.00" sign outside. I was accompanied by the glamorous companion's equally glamorous daughter but, it turned out, to no avail. I don't know if the GS recognised me from the last visit, but his greeting was equally cheery.

"Too late," O'Toole growled when we tried to order lunch. "Finished serving."

I pointed out that it was now actually 1.50 and the notice claimed 2.00 for last orders.

"Hurrumph," he said. "The chef's gone home."

What can you say to that ? All I could think of was to wish, out loud, that Lionel Blair should remain as PM for ever, and we left.

But this was well off the summit of Somerset pub anti-hospitality. On the way back from a Sunday evening visit to the muddy coast of Bridgwater Bay we decided a quick pint was in order. The village pub we came to was less than pretty but looked acceptable in a rough and ready kind of way. There were a few cars parked outside, but the front door was locked. Hearing some sounds of revelry from around the back, we tried going round the side. Why not?

Mistake. In the back yard was an array of trestle tables occupied by about fifty carousing barbarians of both sexes. As we headed for the open side-door of the pub, a large, vest-clad savage, complete with a straggly grey pony-tail, got up and ambled towards us.

"Where d'you think you're going," he snarled.

"Into the pub, if it's all the same to you," I replied, in what I hoped were level tones. "It is a pub, isn't it? You know, *public* house?"

"This is a private party, mate. Pub's closed." Things had gone a bit quiet, and half a dozen of the vest-man's chums were standing up and looking rather less than chummy. The grey-beard took me gently by the elbow and we were escorted from the premises.

As we walked, bemused, back to the car, the strains of unusually obscene songs recommenced with renewed vigour. How a small village could muster such a collection of Neanderthals I'll never know. And on a Sunday at that. It certainly wasn't the local W.I.

To be fair, whilst Somerset pubs aren't always as convivial as Dublin hostelries, they are by no means all in the Slaughtered Lamb league. On the way back from a job on the Blackdowns my colleague and I stopped off for a quick pint at a pretty pub at the foot of the hills. We were greeted cheerfully by the dozen or so locals propping up the bar. (This is always a good sign: a bunch of genial locals in the boozer at six o'clock.)

No sooner had we settled down with our drinks, served by a charming landlady, when a terrier sprinted round from behind the bar and began a passionate sexual assault on my leg.

"Little bugger," grinned one of the company. "He've certainly taken a fancy to you."

The lovely landlady, giggling, scampered round the bar and prised the panting terrier away from my boot. "Whoops, sorry." And she gave my knee a friendly squeeze.

Two or three weeks later we called in again. As we walked through the door a number of residents greeted us with recognition. "It's all right," the landlady said, smiling sweetly, "He's locked up out the back." Being recognised, even if it is on account of my sexual attractiveness to dogs, is surely a measure of a good pub. Well worth revisiting.

Another such measure, in my reckoning, is dog-friendliness. By this I don't mean the presence of overtly amorous canines such as my terrier 'friend', but the readiness of the establishment to welcome our four-legged companions, amorous or otherwise. A pub which bans dogs is a non-starter for me, so a place near the coast which is almost aggressively dog-friendly is a real favourite.

Two notices propped beside the door make their intentions clear. One, featuring a picture of a squiffy-looking dog holding a glass of wine, says "Dogs Welcome" in bold letters. The other, a little more discreet, states "Muddy Dogs (and boots) Welcome". Inside, among the perhaps regrettable hunting paraphernalia, are numerous paintings of sporting hounds of all sorts. This is a dog pub all right.

I've visited this place regularly over the past few years, always accompanied by my dog so, when I turned up without him, the genial landlord naturally enquired as to his whereabouts. When I explained that the old boy had died, the good landlord offered me a trial with a recently 'rescued' hound he had acquired.

"She needs a real good home," he explained, "and she's not getting enough attention here. We're just too busy." The following day I met this beautiful deerhound lurcher and took her home on a fortnight's trial. Needless to say, we hit it off, and she has been my faithful, if somewhat lawless, companion ever since. So, I can truly claim that I got my dog from a man in a pub. She is, of course, Roxie the Longdog.

Not all good Somerset pubs dispense dogs as well as beer, of course, but you never know your luck.

Mendip to the Coast

Harptree Hill to Burrington Combe

With Howard

It's remarkable how difficult it can be to find a dog-friendly taxi in parts of rural Somerset. The plan was to drive to Harptree Hill, walk as far as we could along the Mendip border then get a taxi back to the car, but no taxi was available. (Hint here for four-wheeled entrepreneurs in the Mendip area.) So, once again, we were reduced to a two-car hop, leaving Howard's car in Blagdon and driving mine to Harptree Hill, where we parked where we finished up last time, and headed off west on what promised to be another hot day, even at Mendip altitudes.

The tree-lined lane followed the border westwards along the top of the ridge, the high hedges offering a bit of shade as well as obscuring the view to the north. We managed to miss the concealed footpath which tracks the border as it turns north, so we continued along the lane through blessedly shady, deep woodland until a cleared, grassy field on our left revealed an impressively complete stone circle, about thirty yards across. The map shows the area to be dotted with ancient tumuli, but the neatness of this little circle suggested more recent construction, and we wondered what jolly druidic rituals take place here on the solstices, and who the participants might be.

At Hazel Corner we were confronted by Hazel Lodge, a peculiarly unattractive little building with odd roof elevations and an incongruous picket fence, and here we turned north on a footpath along the drive of what was once Hazel Manor. This was yet another 19th century Gothic pile, having burned down in the 1930's leaving only the lodge as evidence of its existence. We were now on a section of the Limestone Link Trail which, as its name suggests, links the limestone area of Mendip with the Cotswolds some 30 miles away to the north-east.

Leaving the lime-tree-lined drive we turned westwards parallel to the border through dense plantation woodland along what is labelled as a permissive path, the Right of Way having been wrestled from the Forestry Commission by a determined local campaign only a few years ago. At the end of the wood a dog's-leg took us to a deep, overgrown track where an elegant Spotted Wood butterfly danced among the bramble flowers, and blue Damselflies darted and hovered. The marauding horse-flies were far less welcome, taking advantage of exposed legs and arms, but our reflexes proved to be still pretty sharp, and the body-count rose as we crossed Ubley Drove and continued along Leaze Lane. From here we got our first uninterrupted view of the bays and promontories of Blagdon Lake down below, with the Bristol Channel and the hills of Wales far off in the distance. The massive bulk of Mendip was under our feet and, once again, we had that 'on top of the world' feeling we have enjoyed so often on this border patrol, from the Brendons and Exmoor, across the Blackdowns to the rolling heights of the east. Who needs the Lake District?

Back on the border we followed a metalled lane to join a narrow road labelled on the map as Two Trees and began the descent towards Blagdon. Half way down, just over the border, we spotted a small, scrubby area which has been levelled to accommodate a picnic table and a couple of benches, giving marvellous views over the lake and beyond, so we stopped for a lunch break. A bronze plaque here celebrates fifty years of the Blagdon Womens' Institute (bless 'em), founded in 1948, and we wondered what the worthy ladies of those days would have made of the modern movement, in which my daughter Katie organised and ran the Somerset WI's first-ever tea and cake tent at the 2015 Glastonbury Festival just a week ago. Comfortably combining multi-coloured hair, tattoos and nose rings with jam and Jerusalem, these young and not-so-young Somerset ladies went down a storm. Respect!

The lake was shimmering in the heat, Roxie lay flat out in the shade under a tree, and troops of butterflies, including a beautiful Marbled White, were dancing over the swaying grasses, but we had to be on our way. We should have headed back up the hill to follow the border westward again, but that little blue tankard symbol tempted us once more, so we roused ourselves for the short descent into Blagdon. The Seymour Arms is dog-friendly, cool and, most important right now, open. I hesitated over the cider, and the charming young barmaid offered us a taste of Orchard Pig on tap. This hails from near Glastonbury but, I fear, the company has 'gone commercial' in a rather big way since I last encountered it, so we settled for a pint of good Butcombe ale, brewed only a couple of miles away in Wrington. (This is just over the border in the so-called North Somerset, but it's near enough.) The brewery is, itself, a pretty big outfit these days but, somehow, beer seems to cope with up-scaling rather better than cider does in most cases.

Venturing boldly again into the blazing sun we climbed back up the hill a little way before turning west over a stone-slab steeplechase stile alongside a converted chapel and headed across gently sloping fields to the green cool of Fuller's Hay. This lovely old wood, with a diversity of mature trees including lofty limes, perhaps derives its name from Fullers' Earth, a clay mineral used for de-greasing wool and once mined around here. (Or it may have once belonged to a Mr Fuller?) The slope falling away below us is much steeper here, and a deep and narrow combe, almost a miniature gorge, cuts down to the north to give a glimpse of the sun-sparkled lake through the trees.

Emerging from the cool of the wood into the slamming heat of the open fields, the flagging Roxie spotted a cattle trough and drank her fill, taking advantage of her height to reach the water with ease. We plodded on through the knee-high grass, supposedly toward Burrington, and I can only blame the brain-scrambling heat for causing me to reject the clearly marked bridleway. As it was, with some surprise, we found ourselves on the A368 at Rickford, still about a mile north of the border. Luckily, a well-used path presented itself, so we crossed more grassy fields to Burrington where we turned sharp left at the church and began the steep climb back to the border and our return trip to the car. This was tough going at this late stage in the day, but the woods afforded some shade until we emerged into the fields. Then it was a long haul up steep, open fields where the grazing is barely keeping the heathland flora at bay, eventually reaching the little carpark at the head of Burrington Combe, only a few yards away from the border. A bit of woodland, part of the Burrington Ham nature reserve, offered some shade before we were out in the open again across a couple of fields leading to the oddly-named Luvers Lane, where a gentle breeze and the glorious views made it all worthwhile, and bearable.

At this point Howard's mobile phone began to make noises, so we stopped in the shade of a small tree while he wrestled with what seemed to be an unfamiliar piece of technology. After no small effort we attempted to decipher a more or less incomprehensible text message, apparently from his dear wife, possibly enquiring as to our time of return. I left him attempting a reply while I accompanied Roxie on a fruitless rabbit hunt along the hedgerow, finally subsiding under another tree to await the telecommunicator. After what seemed like a long time Howard reappeared, and I asked if he had been texting a full account of the day's events but, "No", he assured me, with Yorkshire brevity. "I told her we'd be back after six."

We strolled down Rhodyate Hill for the second time to retrieve Howard's car, then drove back to mine on Harptree Hill where the 'Welcome to Somerset' sign saw us safely back over the border. The homeward drive over the high heathland and down the Steeps to Wells was a fitting end to a hard but glorious day over Mendip, while the Longdog slept across the back seat with her feet in the air.

Burrington Combe to Rowberrow

With Lorna and The Twins

It seemed like a long trek 'up north', but we got there in the end and turned off the A368 and drove up the narrow, rocky gorge which is Burrington Combe: almost a miniature Cheddar Gorge but without the neon signs, cheese shops and other tourist paraphernalia. We passed the famous Rock of Ages (cleft for me?) and up, past steep outcrops apparently housing Elephant's, Lionel's and Toad's Holes as well as glaringly white goats perching on the ledges. Parking at the top we donned our rain-gear, Roxie resplendent in her sleek, fluorescent yellow, and crossed the border back into Somerset for a short climb to join the Limestone Link heading west. The view to the north is obstructed by trees, but above us to the south a sea of bracken rose up and rolled away over the hilltop as we followed the contour around this massive shoulder of Mendip. The extent and density of the bracken invasion came as a surprise, as I'm sure I remember this area being proper heathland, with heather and blueberries and the like, in the not-too-distant past. Clearly the control measures now being employed on Quantock and parts of Exmoor have not been applied here, leaving the bracken blanket to smother the former inhabitants to the detriment of wildlife and grazing alike.

The Twins (our nine-year-old grandsons) spotted some striking lichens on the rocks exposed along our path. These had the look of typical crustose Xanthoria types, but were marked with broken, more or less concentric circles in black, giving an impression of a Bengal tiger's face! It's nice to have a couple of pairs of alert young eyes to pick up these delightful details which could so easily pass unnoticed under a grown-up boot. The path is now following the border as it descends into the steep-sided gully which contains East Twin Brook, a fitting name in view of our company today. The brook itself was almost dry after a prolonged rain-free spell, which reminded us that the rain had stopped, allowing the removal of waterproofs from man, twins and dog with universal relief. Suitably liberated we crossed the course of the brook over great limestone slabs and climbed out of this deep, tree-lined mini-gorge to gain our first real view of the day as the steeper hillside fell away below us. In the foreground the many-coloured patchwork of fields was interspersed with a thick scattering of hamlets and villages (Bristol dormitory-land?) and, in the distance, the Channel running between the coastal plain and the cloud-topped Welsh hills beyond: yet another magnificent Mendip vista.

As we marched through the bracken, alternately marvelling at the view and checking bare legs for ticks, we encountered our first walkers of the day: a rather morose couple with a brace of friendly Springers and a longdog. In appearance the latter could be a close cousin of Roxie, though this one seemed as morose as its human companions, perhaps on account of its short lead and muzzle! An unusual hound to require a muzzle. Shame.

Looking across to the other side of Burrington Combe, only a couple of hundred yards away over this pretty little gorge, the fissured strata of the limestone outcrops are so regular as to look like huge dry-stone walls. As with so many places in Somerset the geology here is an endless source of variety and wonder.

We lost the view as we descended sharply down to West Twin Brook where Roxie lapped a quick drink from the little water trickling down the gully between the rocks. There is something almost tropical about these deep and narrow little combes, and we paused for a moment to imagine what they would look like when full with a winter torrent. Reverie over, we pressed on, and continued along the contour to a major junction of paths where the bracken of Black Down meets the dense woodland of Rowberrow Warren. Here, we stepped around a veritable multi-cultural gathering of rather uncommunicative young people resting on the grass, some of them cowering away from our ever-friendly hound. We turned south to ascend the shoulder of Black Down for our return trip to the car.

The steep, well-worn path runs up alongside a deep gully bordering the woodland, the Twins bounding around like mountain goats while we slightly older ones adopted a more sedate, steady pace. At the top we spotted a small herd of North Devon cattle, complete with fetching, down-curved horns, up to their shoulders in the bracken. They regarded us with benign interest as we passed within a few yards of them, and I was bound to wonder again about those frequent stories of cattle attacking dogs and their companions, sometimes with fatal results. I have had dealings with cattle and cattle-men all my life and have yet to come across any incidents of truly aggressive bovines, with the obvious exceptions of frustrated bulls and protective mothers. Certainly, bunches of heifers and bullocks will show a keen interest in dogs and people, but I have never known them to be more than curious or playful and, thankfully, these placid Devons were no exception.

Turning back eastward along the top of Black Down we passed a herd of Exmoor ponies peering over the bracken, then skirted the trig point on Beacon Batch (325m) to be confronted by the most expansive view yet. With a sweep of more than 180° from south west, through north to east we could see Brean Down poking out into the Channel, Weston-super-Mare, Steep Holm and Flat Holm, both Severn bridges, Blagdon and Chew Valley lakes and bits of Bristol in the distance. And could that be the Malvern Hills way up to the north? With the possible exception of Dunkery Beacon on a clear day this must be one of the most spectacular viewpoints in Somerset.

A gentle stroll down the hillside took us back to the car at the top of Burrington Combe, and here we tried to decide on a campaign strategy for the afternoon. Lunch called loud and clear, so we headed for the nearest pub (according to the map) at Shipham. Judging from previous experience it should have come as no surprise that it was closed, but we were heartened by a sign indicating a farm-shop and café, with a mention of cider. This stirred distant memories of a cider-farm we used to visit in a previous incarnation, so we continued up the hill out of Shipham and, lo and behold, there it was. The present manifestation is a far cry from the open-fronted barn we once knew, now appearing as a mixture of camp-site, farm-shop, café and, by the look of the large, rough-gravelled car park, truck-stop. In former times, when we lived in the Gordano valley (then still part of Somerset-proper), a short Sunday morning drive would bring us up here to find the venerable Mr Lukins dispensing cider and cheese from his barn. Sitting regally on a straw bale he would offer generous tastings of both to his delighted customers, the whole place embodying the atmosphere of a rural tavern in a by-gone age. Things are rather different now, but the café is still able to provide excellent cider, made on another farm just down the hill in Shipham, and hearty sandwiches to order. The young lady behind the counter was far too young to have been around in the 'good old days' but, when I mentioned my recollections, she told me that 'the old chap' , long gone, alas, is something of a legend hereabouts, his exploits including burying barrels of cider around the farm to evade the attentions of the excise men. Happy days.

Refreshed and invigorated we drove back to the Rowberrow turn-off and squeezed the car under a hedge along the lane before descending a steep path through ancient woodland leading down to the border in the bottom of the valley. Huge beech and ash trees, an unusual combination, towered over us, their gnarled roots grappling with the limestone outcrops along the path. Heading eastwards back toward the point where we turned back before lunch, the path follows the boggy course of a stream through the narrow gorge, with a mixture of natural and plantation woodland cladding the steep sides, making for an almost Tolkienesque atmosphere. The moss-crowned remains of extensive and substantial dry-stone walls flank the path, presumably marking the boundaries of the manor way up above us in Rowberrow.

As we neared the end of the woodland and the point on the border we reached earlier, excited barking led us to a young man with a couple of dogs, one a tail-wagging Labrador pup and the other a lively West Highland which had been optimistically chasing deer in the woods. While they exchanged enthusiastic greetings with Roxie, their companion kindly suggested a return route which would keep us in Somerset and avoid an unnecessary climb. Gratefully, we accepted the alternative and turned back across a cleared, bracken-covered hillside towards Rowberrow in brilliant sunshine. These cleared areas, now managed by the Forestry Commission, must provide some interesting habitats, perhaps for Adders, Nightjars and other denizens of forest clearings like this.

Joining the road, we climbed out of the valley and passed prettily-maintained cottages interspersed with large, imposing houses set back in extensive gardens. The affluence of this area was probably founded on mining, as with many such places on Mendip, this one being mostly zinc ores including calamine. Whilst affording great wealth to some, the mining industry also ensured extreme poverty for the hapless workers in the 18th and 19th centuries. This area was so renowned for its barbarism that William Wilberforce, no less, was involved in improving the lot of the peasantry hereabouts with the provision of a school and other civilising facilities. The savagery of the population in those days has been attributed to the toxic effects of the heavy metals associated with the mining of lead and zinc, and to this day the levels of cadmium in the soil near Shipham are the highest in the country. It was long believed that vegetation grown on these soils was toxic to humans and livestock, but recent research suggests that uptake by plants is minimal so Mendip residents can eat their produce in safety. Probably.

Just short of our starting point we passed the church of St Michael and All Angels which was founded in the 14th century and extensively rebuilt in 1865 with typical 19th century pomp. It sports an unusual rounded turret attached to one corner of the tower, probably housing a staircase. I doubt that the church was ever frequented by Rowberrow's most famous resident: the author and confirmed humanist Terry Pratchett lived here between 1970 – 93, writing some of his best-known works during that time. Surely these deep, wooded valleys and soaring hills inspired some of the landscapes in Mr Pratchett's intricate fantasy novels.

Back at the car the two nine-year-olds were as bouncy as when we started, though the same couldn't truthfully be said for at least one of their grandparents and Roxie, who collapsed across the back seat of the car with her feet in the air yet again. Another great day on Mendip.

Interlude 8

Somerset Kids

In a previous incarnation I was a science teacher here in rural Somerset. Fortunately, it was sufficiently long ago for the kids not to have been homogenised by the so-called 'electronic age', so there were still some real characters to be found in the classroom. Some of my fondest memories are of the supposed 'lower' sets, in which the kids still spoke with a local accent almost impenetrable to outsiders.

Ant'ny was a classic of his kind. Short and stocky, with a shock of curly hair over a round, freckled face, he was the epitome of the farm boys for whom school was a regrettable interlude in their rural lives. With fore-arms like hams terminating in huge red hands it was obvious that he was more at ease with a dung-fork than with a pen, but Ant'ny was interested in biology. The reproductive activities of earthworms clearly fascinated him, and as I described the hermaphroditic process employed by these lowly annelids his attention was absolute. When I'd finished his big red hand shot up.

"Now then," he said, "are you sayin' that they worms do it to *each other*, like, *at the same time?*"

"That's it, Ant'ny," I said. "That's just what they do."

He shook his head slowly, in admiration. "Well, I'm buggered," he said reverently. This was one of the few examples of real revelation I ever saw in the classroom

Such was his interest in living things that he made some effort to get to grips with the subject and produced some more or less respectable test results. On one occasion, when I returned a test paper, he and his desk-mate examined their marks with interest. His companion compared their results and turned to me in outraged disbelief.

"'Ere, sir," he complained, "how come he've got 45 and I've only got 15?"

Ant'ny sniffed with appropriate contempt. "'Cos you're a daft bugger Parsons, that's why," he growled. Out of the mouths of babes and Somerset country boys ….

Ant'ny's presence also contributed positively to classroom management. Following a minor misdemeanour by one of his classmates I was obliged to point out that any further time-wasting would result in the extension of this, the last lesson of the day, to make up for lost time. As Ant'ny travelled home by coach to his rural outpost this was a serious threat.

With no reference to me he turned slowly in his seat and pointed a stubby finger at the offender.

"And if that do happen, my son," he said gravely, "thees'll be taking I home by piggy-back." Matter settled.

Elsewhere I've talked about the difficulty of describing, let alone defining, the Somerset character. For me, these rural adolescents represented what was once characteristic of the county. While formal schooling was rarely to their liking, they showed a quick wit and down-to-earth practicality that outshone some of their more 'academic' peers. Many of them certainly had an appreciation and enjoyment of real life so lacking in modern times.

I met another former member of Ant'ny's class in a pub a few years later. After the usual warm greetings, I asked what he was up to and how he was getting on.

"On the farm, o'course," he grinned. "I been daggin' today. Brilliant. Best job on the farm. They look beautiful when they'm done."

For the uninitiated, dagging is the skilful process of trimming the mucky wool from the rear-end of a sheep, nowadays accomplished with electric shears. And the boy is right. The neat, clean look of a freshly dagged sheep is a joy. The long tails of hill sheep look like crew-cut sausages. Lovely.

Not all of my former pupils were as sharp or motivated as some of the farm lads of course. An exasperated colleague once asked a sullen, uncooperative boy in an art class if there was *anything* he liked doing.

"Yep," answered the lad seriously. "Going up the den, smokin' fags and drinking cider." Points for honesty if nothing else.

Which is not to suggest that all Somerset kids are genial rustics with straw in their hair. When I was teaching I was once presented with a charming young man whose family had recently moved to the area following what I gathered to be a bit of a financial disaster. He had formerly attended a well-known independent school, as was attested by his 'cultured' accent and pleasantly urbane manner. The problem was in constructing his time-table, and circumstances were such that I had to explain to him that the only biology class available within the constraints was what we were then allowed to call a 'bottom' set.

"The trouble is," I said, "this group isn't terribly academic. In fact, to be honest old chap, some of them can barely read and write."

He beamed cheerfully. "Actually, sir, neither can I, so there's no problem, is there?"

This same likeable lad later completed the arduous Ten Tors training and expedition, clad throughout in a complete Barbour suit, the weight of which would tax a hardened squaddie. As they say these days, Respect!

Another favourite was a boy whose father was a retired colonel but who had clearly failed to inherit any military inclinations. He was, perhaps, a little over-weight and ponderous, and insisted on maintaining his straight, blond hair at shoulder-blade length. What with that, and his interest in art, mathematics and Dungeons and Dragons, he was sometimes the subject of generally good-natured teasing by his peers. But on one occasion they went too far.

He was sent to me, as his form master, in disgrace, accused of an act of extreme violence against one of his fellows. Amazed at this totally uncharacteristic behaviour, I demanded an explanation.

"Well, sir, it was like this. It was in the art room, and he had some scissors and he was going to cut my hair."

"And ….?"

"So, I turned round and, well, I head-butted him, sir. And I'm afraid I broke his nose."

Once again, Respect! In the circumstances I felt a stern reprimand was adequate, and it was pleasing to note that the head-butting artist was never bullied again.

Which just goes to show, as my old granny used to say, the diversity of Somerset kids. I only hope they remain so.

Star to Loxton

With Lizzie

I have bemoaned before the difficulty of finding dog-friendly taxis in the north of the County, but this time I found a happy exception. The lady at Sandford Private Hire assured me that there would be no problem with a dog, nor with the fact that I am more than a little vague about the time and place of our pick-up. "Just give him a ring", she said. "It'll be fine."

A border purist (obsessive?) would insist on starting on the border at the top of the hill above Churchill where we finished up last time, but a walk down the A38 to get to the appropriate footpath looks like a short-cut to suicide, so we opted to start from the village of Star just down the road. This allowed for a heavy-duty breakfast at the Star Inn which, we hoped, would compensate for a likely lack of lunch on what may well be a drastically pub-deficient route. Roxie was well pleased with this dog-friendly road house where she enjoyed her share of sausage and bacon while reclining like a Roman gourmand.

Our starting footpath is directly opposite the Star, climbing steeply south-eastwards over what Lizzie informed me is 'gruffy ground', the humpy, bumpy remains of haphazard old mine workings. Such was the scattering of mineral outcrops that the free-lance miners dug wherever they could, seemingly at random, leaving humps and hollows which, now grassed over, are of little use except for rough grazing. We topped the hillside and joined the road just north of Shipham, walking down alongside intermittent and only moderately dangerous traffic into the village. A white cat with no ears came within a few yards of certain mortality, but Lizzie's vegetarian tranquillity seemed to calm the lead-straining Roxie, who soon lost interest in the first potential prey of the day.

Finding the right footpath out of the village to join the border proved less than straightforward as there appeared to be at least four leading in roughly the required direction. I can see in retrospect that the loop we opted for is hardly justified, leading us only to a short section of north/south border before we were obliged by lack of Right of Way to turn back onto the West Mendip Way. The consolation was that our detour afforded Lizzie the opportunity to try out a makeshift swing hanging irresistibly from the branch of a sturdy oak alongside the path.

This central section of western Mendip is marked by relatively small, steep hills, and we skirted one of these, Winterhead Hill, on the West Mendip Way heading back to the border. We then descended over grazed fields to meet the track from Winterhead Hill Farm. It was wedding day, and a procession of beribboned cars passed us with many cheery waves, presumably heading for an outdoor reception somewhere up on the hill. If you ever get to read this, Alex and Lucy, (your names were on a sign at the junction) may I say you made a very handsome couple.

The West Mendip Way crosses the border into North Somerset, but a footpath allowed us to stay with the border, turning south up a steep, deep, wooded gully, opening out into a huge field occupied by a large herd of black cattle, including a handsome bull. The white horns of the cows and their elegant conformation distinguish them from the Aberdeen Angus so popular elsewhere in Somerset, and mark them out as Welsh Blacks, a hardy breed which hails from the very hills we can see over the water. The bull, comfortingly hornless, eyed us with total indifference. (It may be worth a mention that bulls over 10 months old of *dairy* breeds may not be kept on land crossed by public Rights of Way, whereas bulls of *beef* breeds, such as these Welsh Blacks, are permitted as long as they are accompanied by a sufficiency of cows or heifers. I trust the reason for the latter proviso is self-explanatory!)

The exit from this field was barred by a chained and padlocked gate impassable to a Longdog, so we circumnavigated with a bit of gentle fence-bending to allow her through. Only when we turned 90° west to follow the border along Callow Drove did we notice the alternative exit, a stone-slab stile, but this too was protected by a dog-proof fence. While these little obstructions are annoying I am bound to have some sympathy with the farmer whose beautiful and valuable cattle may be put at risk by careless walkers leaving gates open. Besides, neither landowners nor local authorities are obliged in law to provide easy access for dogs, though perhaps they should be?

The Drove is as wide as a road, a testament to its name and former use, and flanked by crumbling dry-stone walls, but the long, mostly untrodden grass showed little sign of much recent activity. A pair of roe deer in their bright orange summer coats trotted away unhurriedly across the field on the other side of the wall, blissfully unaware of Roxie, as she was of them. Through gaps in the wall on the north side we could see the by-now expected expansive views rolling away into the distance.

We began the steady descent down Shute Shelve Hill, the site of public executions in days gone by. It is hard to imagine such ghastly scenes in such a beautiful place, but today the tranquillity was broken not by the howls of the mob but by the growl of the traffic on the A38 immediately below. Finishing the descent through an overgrown coppice we hit the road at a convenient pedestrian island which allowed us to cross in relative safety to continue westward along the border and rejoin the West Mendip Way.

A small car-park marks the entrance to King's Wood, though which king originally claimed ownership is not clear. Now managed by the National Trust, the wood, at least the upper sections along the border, is made up mostly of big Ash and Sweet Chestnut and, apparently, the rare Small-leaved Lime, which we failed to find. We stopped for a minimal picnic at the edge of the wood, then ventured out into bright sunshine and a stiff head-wind as we approached the heights of Wavering Down. From the trig point on the Down (211m), surrounded only by close-cropped grass and the ever-increasing bracken, the view is nothing short of stupendous, with a barely interrupted sweep of 360°. In addition to the familiar vista to the west and north we now had Axbridge reservoir below us to the south, with Glastonbury Tor in the hazy distance, and we needed no crystals or dream-catchers to feel the real magic here. We were not particularly high, even by Somerset standards, (Wills Neck on the Quantocks is 386m and Dunkery Beacon on Exmoor is 519m) but the low-lying Levels to the south and the floodplain of the Severn to the west and north give the impression of greater altitude and distance here.

For the last couple of miles we were following the border along a beautiful, straight dry-stone wall, clearly recently restored. These walls are a prominent feature of the high-Mendip landscape where hedges will grow only under protest on the exposed heights. The building began in medieval times when farmers cleared the stones from the shallow, rocky soil. The stones were put to the best possible use. Wall building reached its peak in the 18th and 19th centuries when the Enclosure Acts and plentiful, cheap labour allowed their rapid expansion. In recent times their value as a landscape feature and as a rare mini-habitat for a specialised flora has been recognised, and funding has been available for their restoration and maintenance. We are fortunate, indeed, to have craftsmen still on hand to do the job.

Rounding the craggy top of Crook Peak we left the wall and the border and descended towards the roaring M5 through a dense hazel coppice onto a tarmac lane. This leads to a bridge over the motorway where we paused, briefly, to note our crossing of the border and to watch the Saturday afternoon traffic howling past below us. The speed and volume of this ghastly procession was in brutal contrast to the peace of the hills we had just left, and it was a relief to press on and leave behind this hideous symbol of modern life. Surprisingly, Roxie was unmoved by the noise and the odd proximity of the traffic down below us and viewed it all with a marked lack of interest.

In North Somerset again, we took a neatly-cropped footpath across a couple of fields to the little village of Loxton, where we summoned our taxi by way of the miracle of mobile telephone. As the lady had promised, the cheery proprietor was soon on the scene and had no trouble accommodating a Longdog on a plump dog-bed under his capacious hatch. Back at the Star, we commiserated with the landlord about the iniquities of 'tied' houses and how they limit the availability of local beverages and settled for a pint of some dubious Irish beer. But in the golden afternoon sunshine in the garden we could forget the provenance of the ale and could enjoy the tail-end of another inspiring, elevated border trail day.

Loxton to Bleadon Bridge

With Pete

This one is a short hop and a fill-in, and a bit of a recce in preparation for the Last Lap to the end of the border at the coast. From just south of Loxton the border follows the middle of the River Axe all the way to the Bristol Channel at the eastern end of Brean Down where our round-the-border trek began. I had hoped to complete this last stage by boat along the middle of the river, but the presence of sluices and the absence of suitable boats rather scuppered this fanciful idea. Unfortunately, footpaths are lacking on the Somerset side so we were forced onto the 'other' side where a pretty uneventful road leads from Loxton to Shiplate Manor Farm.

A footpath turns south off the road then west following the river, which is a couple of hundred yards to the south of us and hidden from view by a maize field. This awful stuff not only obscures the view but offers little scope for wildlife and has the potential to impoverish the soil into the bargain. As it is used to make a form of silage it also furthers the iniquitous practice of keeping cattle indoors for most or all of the year. And these factory-farmers, or agri-businessmen as they should more accurately be known, have the audacity to blame badgers for the high incidence of bovine TB, when they have their cattle banged up shoulder to shoulder in a bovine

Cider with Roxie

slammer. Why the Government panders to these people and their nonsensical badger cull is a complete mystery.

Leaving the maize behind we crossed a couple of small, grassy fields complete with a few handsome Devon Reds blissfully grazing as cattle should, before we turned south, crossing a stout steel bridge over the river and into Somerset. A pair of swans with a brace of downy cygnets were grazing on the duckweed blanketing the surface of the still water, this once-tidal waterway now being tamed by a couple of sluices between here and the estuary. Looking north and east, the tail-end of Mendip runs down to Bleadon, and to the south the flat infinity of the Levels stretches away into the haze. And so along the river to Bleadon Bridge, where the last leg of this border journey will begin.

It would be a shame to leave Bleadon without some mention of its history, even though it's now on the 'wrong' side of the river. Its moment of glory came in the 8th century when the Viking raiders were camped on Steepholm. I can do no better than quote the words of Mr Gibbons who recorded this tale from local sources in 1670:

"THEIR FIFTH INVASION WAS AT UPHILL, BLEDON, ETC., WHERE I HAVE ENQUIRED OF THE INHABITANTS WHETHER THEY HAD AT ANY TIME HEARD OF ANY DEANES THAT CAME IN THE DAYES OF YORE TO STEEP HOMES NEAR THEM. "THEY TOLD ME THAT THE GENERALL TRADITION OF THEIR COUNTRY HATH BEENE THAT A FLEETE OF DEANES FLED TO SHELTER THEMSELVES IN THE SAID ISLE, AND SOMTIME THEY BRAKE OUT INTO ENGLAND AND SOMETIMES INTO WALES FOR SUSTENANCE. "AT LENGTH COMING TO UPHILL AND BLEDON THEY FASTENED THEIR SHIPS TO THE SHOARE, LEFT THEM AND MARCHED UP INTO THE COUNTRY FOR BOOTIES, AND THAT ALL THE INHABITANTS FLED WAY BEFORE THEM, ONE POOR LAME WOMAN EXCEPTED, WHICH HID IN A ROCK NEAR THE SHIPS. WHEN SHE WAS NEAR SPENT WITH HUNGER SHE WAS NECESSITATED TO ADVENTURE DOWN TO THE SHIPS FOR RELIEF, SAYING TO HERSELF, WITH THE LEPERS, 'IF THEY KILL ME, I SHALL BUT DIE'. "BUT COMING THITHER AND SEARCHING FROM SHIP TO SHIP, AND FINDING NO LIVING CREATURE, AT LAST ESPYING AN HATCHET, SHE TOOK IT, AND WITH IT CHOPPED OFF ALL THE CABLES WHICH ANCHORED THE SHIPS TO THE SHOARE, AND SENT THEM TO SEA WHERE

THEY QUICKLY PERISHED. "THE DANES HAVING GOTTEN INTELLIGENCE OF THE LOSS OF SOME OF THEIR SHIPS, SPEEDILY RETREATED, TO SAVE THEMSELVES AND THE REST, BUT THE PEOPLE OF THE COUNTRY, HAVING INTELLIGENCE THAT ALL THEIR SHIPS WERE CAST AWAY, TOOK COURAGE, PURSUED THEM TO BLEDON, THERE FOUGHT, AND DESTROYED THEM WITH SUCH BLOODY SLAUGHTER, AS THAT FROM THENCE THE PLACE TOOK, AND EVERSINCE HATH KEPT, THE NAME BLEDON, ALIAS BLEED-DOWN OR BLOUD-DOWN, TO THIS DAY."

Another example of the folly of tangling with Somersetians.

Bleadon to Uphill

With Geoff, Ginny, Lorna, Matti & Alexius

The Last Lap, and an Anglo/Irish/Dutch expedition to boot.

We left the cars near Bleadon Bridge with both the Somerset and North Somerset border signs in view, making us technically in no-man's land? Regrettably this last leg of my round-the-border walk has to be in North Somerset, in sight of but on the 'wrong' side of the border due to a woeful lack of Rights of Way on the Somerset side.

While planning the route for today I noticed, on the map, a track running along the west bank of the River Axe (the Somerset side): not a public right of way, alas, but a track nevertheless. Naturally, I attempted to gain permission to walk the track, but without success. The first of the three farms along the route was, in fact, a caravan park, and whilst the owner was happy for me to walk his section he warned me that the other two, still farming in the midst of caravan-land, might be less accommodating, and he was right. The very friendly wife of the second land-owner explained that her husband would definitely not allow such a venture as he was constantly plagued by trespassing holidaymakers wandering about over his land with scant regard for the country code. Besides, she continued, the third farmer was a "cantankerous old bugger who said no to everything", so the west bank route was clearly a non-starter. North Somerset it would have to be.

Just to the north of Bleadon Bridge we took a footpath westward along the river bank. The water was remarkably clear and still, well coated with bright green duckweed and almost lapping our feet, with little clearings where patient fishermen waited behind their long poles. This was a glorious sunny morning with just a few puffy clouds high up, the whole scene having a strangely peaceful, timeless feel. I released Roxie, and she loped ahead with her nose to the ground, perhaps seeking out the remains of the fishermen's bait. Still close to the water we followed the path as it passed from a field of close-cut grass to a stand of towering maize, a harsh contrast to the flat serenity of the almost lake-like river. The angular, rustling nastiness of this uniform, soulless crop symbolises, for me, the mechanised industry which is modern farming. It will be cut and pulverised by massive, nightmare machines then fed to cattle confined indoors, and I am reminded of those vast, empty fields we walked through down in the south a few weeks ago: inevitable, perhaps, but awful nonetheless.

The path leaves the river and cuts 'inland', the way-markers notable by their absence. (This North Somerset lot should take a lesson from Mendip District over the border where the way-markers rarely let us down.) We made a map-based guess and crossed a playing field attached to a chalet site, then turned north to join what we assumed to be a little-used road which would lead us back towards the river where we intended to take a bridleway across Bleadon Level. Our naïve expectation of a quiet stroll along the tarmac was rapidly shattered by an intermittent stream of cars in both directions with an occasional coach and lorry for good measure. Close perusal of the map revealed that this must be a devious short-cut from the A370 to the holiday hell of Brean and Berrow, and I am bound to sympathise again with the lady farmer who bemoaned the annual invasion of holidaymakers with, she told me, 50,000 of them at the height of the season. The Vikings could hardly have been more devastating than this lot.

Crossing Summerways Bridge we turned south onto a long, potentially lethal straight, dodging into gateways to avoid the worst of the traffic. To be fair to the 'visitors' - and it is not difficult to tell that they are visitors, with their pink skin and strange, colourful clothes - they all gave us a wide berth, perhaps thinking that walking into heavy traffic on a narrow lane with a large dog is some quaint local custom or initiation rite. With more than a little relief we reached our bridleway and turned off westwards, applauding as we passed the notice displayed in the gateway: "The Countryside is not your Personal Dumping Ground. Use the Tip like a Normal Person. Punishment: £5000 fine or 5 Years Inside."   Harsh but fair, we thought, but possibly not an official Council notice?

Bleadon Level is flat and low (6-7m according to the map), made up of boggy fields divided by rhynes marked with lines of Phragmites reeds. A cluster of Canada Geese and a single hovering Kestrel were the only signs of life in what might well be a bleak landscape on a duller day. As it is, the brassy mid-day sun gave it an illusory air of permanence and stillness, despite the ranks of caravan roofs we could see across the water in the distance. We paused for a brief refreshment break, but the lack of shade was clearly not to Roxie's liking as she tried to burrow under a hedge to get out of the sun, so we pressed on. A couple of small wooden 'houses' on tall poles must be Kestrel nesting-boxes, much like the ones we saw in Holland years ago. These, the marshy lowlands and the remains of an ancient windmill we could see in the distance up ahead must be a reminder of home for our Dutch contingent.

The track curves around the less-than-picturesque bulk of Weston sewage works before joining the tarmac near its entrance. A new pathway along the river bank, not shown on the map, was tempting, but the lack of shade persuaded us towards the 'inland' route where the way-marking was, again, less than definitive.   After some discussion we made our way across the Bleadon Levels Nature Reserve, crossed a couple of grassy fields and emerged at the back end of Uphill marina under an impressive cliff.   A group of youngsters enjoying instruction in the art of rock-climbing reminded me of a course I took here, on these very same faces, long ago in a former incarnation.

A dog-friendly café offered a welcome tea-break, and we engaged in conversation with a fellow Longdog enthusiast before setting out on the last lap of The Last Lap. We left the marina through formidable anti-tide gates, crossed a footbridge and followed the path alongside the pill running across the saltmarsh to the river. The numerous boats drawn up on the mud looked as if they have been there forever, and we wondered how often the tide is high enough to reach them. Not often, by the look of them. Nearing the river, the path turns sharply north towards the mouth of the estuary, and the tide was low, as usual, as we passed the remains of the jetty which once served a ferry across to the Somerset side. The ferry closed as recently as 1980, and in view of the hordes of holidaymakers on both sides of the Axe it seems odd that no plans to restore the ferry service appear to be afoot. The proposed 5-mile cycle path linking Weston with Brean via a bridge over the Brean Cross Sluice seems like a poor alternative and well beyond the endurance potential of many of the holidaymakers we've seen today.

On muddy sand we followed the course of the estuary as far as we could go before the bottomless mud necessitated a halt. This is it: we were as near to the border as we could get, just a few hundred yards short of the tail-end of Brean Down where this circuit of Somerset began. As if in celebration, Roxie relieved herself on the mud in grand style, necessitating some hasty burying before we retreated to drier land for some hugs and hand-shakes and a well-earned bottle of fizz. (More properly we should have celebrated with cider, of course, but carrying sufficient for six was a daunting prospect considering the heat of the day. The cider will certainly come later.)

All that remained was a quick march through Uphill to get the bus back to Bleadon which, if nothing else, afforded me the opportunity to ask a young lady where we might find the Bleadon bus-stop. Low humour, perhaps, but appropriate to the day.

I lament that the last stretch of this round-the-border journey had to be completed on the 'wrong' side but, in a way, it typifies the incongruities and rather haphazard nature of the whole venture. What is there left to say...?

Epilogue

Soon after we finished the Last Lap I began assembling my notes, recordings and so on with a view to getting started on The Book. Unfortunately, I was more than a little distracted when Roxie developed an obvious and persistent limp in her left hind leg. To reduce if not quite to cut a long story short, several visits to the vet, complete with X-rays, resulted in an anticipated but unwelcome diagnosis: a damaged cruciate ligament. The only recommended treatment was a repair operation involving significant quantities of titanium hardware and a good deal of surgical expertise. Our vet is an honest man and advised us to employ the skills of a specialist orthopaedic surgeon based in Exeter. This we did, and while I don't propose to tell you the cost of the exercise, suffice to say that if this little book sells in thousands, not the most likely outcome even if someone can be persuaded to publish it, I shall still be well out of pocket.

While I understood the nature of the operation by way of the vet's lucid explanation, I have to admit to being less clear about the consequences. i.e. One month of close supervision with virtually no exercise at all, followed by another month of two ten-minute on-lead walks per day with close supervision maintained between times. No running, jumping, stair-climbing etc. This to be followed by another month or two of gradually increasing activity until we could be fairly sure that all was well.

All seemed to be going well on the leg front when I noticed that *my* heart beat had suddenly become somewhat irregular. I will cut this bit even shorter: The punchline is that I was diagnosed with a faulty mitral valve which needed surgical fixing. Bloody heart surgery! Me! Not been in hospital since I broke my leg fifty years ago! The upshot was that after some amazing 'Black & Decker' surgery in

Bristol it was my turn for a few weeks convalescence. Now it seems reasonable that this should be the ideal opportunity for a bit of book writing but, alas, this was not to be.

A combination of anaesthesia, analgesics and assorted other drugs seemed to have scrambled my brain so now, nine weeks after the op., is the first time I've felt the urge to tickle the keyboard. This, I hope, is an adequate explanation for the time-lag between finishing the walks and doing anything about it.

If there is any kind of moral to this whole saga it can only be that walking round the border of Somerset buggers up dogs' knees and humans' hearts. Be warned.

People who liked '*CIDER WITH ROXIE*' also liked

REPORTS FROM COASTAL STATIONS

by Geoff Saunders

Acknowledgements

I think 'Acknowledgements' sounds a bit formal and almost grudging, so I prefer to say 'Thanks', and there are plenty of those due.

First, its thanks again to everyone who accompanied me on the walks (all acknowledged in the Cast List. p.13), without whom I would never have started let alone finished, and to all the good people we encountered on the way.

Then its thanks to the 'Production Team' :

I'll readily admit that without the relentless encouragement (badgering?) of Geoff Saunders the book would almost certainly have remained in its original A4 state, consigned to my desk drawer for evermore. Geoff not only undertook the first edit and formatting but ended up sorting out the publishing as well, my main contribution at this stage being the provision of cider.

Special thanks are due to my brother-in-law Bev Blackmore, who is responsible for all the photography as well as the cover design. Bev has the artist's eye for such things.

My thanks for the line drawings go to my 15-year-old grandson Dylan Milton, whose talent speaks for itself.

The final edit and sort-out was heroically undertaken by my daughter, Katie Newell, who had the audacity to make changes and to justify them!

A huge 'thank you' to all of them.

Lastly, a final 'thank you' to Roxie the Longdog, who not only inspired the whole thing but whose name provided what I think is a pretty snappy title.

To complete the acknowledgements, I must credit Laurie Lee for the original inspiration in more ways than one.